THE END OF THE ANCIENT WORLD

THE *END OF THE* ANCIENT WORLD

Santo Mazzarino

TRANSLATED FROM THE ITALIAN BY
George Holmes

19 66

ALFRED · A · KNOPF
NEW YORK

L. C. catalog card number: 64-19092

THIS IS A BORZOI BOOK
PUBLISHED BY ALFRED A. KNOPF, INC.

 Manufactured in the United States of America, and distributed by Random House, Inc. Published simultaneously in Toronto, Canada, by Random House of Canada, Limited.

FIRST AMERICAN EDITION

Originally published in Italian by Aldo Garzanti Editore as *La Fine del Mondo Antico.*

Acknowledgments

For permission to quote from copyright works acknowledgments are due as follows:

Messrs George Allen & Unwin for *The Revolt of the Masses* by Ortega y Gasset; the Clarendon Press for *A Roman Reformer and Inventor* by E. A. Thompson and *Social and Economic History of the Roman Empire* (second edition) by M. Rostovtzeff; the Loeb Classical Library and Harvard University Press for the translation of Petronius; Oxford and Cambridge University Presses for the New English Bible, New Testament, Copyright 1961.

Preface

The aim of this book is twofold: on the one hand to describe the history of the ideas of 'decadence' and the 'death of Rome' as they were understood and transformed from the second century B.C. to our own times; on the other to give a modern interpretation of the fall of the ancient world through criticism and discussion of the various solutions and hypotheses. I believe that, considered from this dual point of view, the theme of the 'death of Rome' has a particular interest. We feel the need both to follow through the development of the ideas of 'decadence' and the 'end' of the ancient world and to consider again on our own account what explanation of this 'end' may appear necessary and sufficient to the man of today. Just for this reason however a 'dialogue' of this kind is inexhaustible and I shall be content if I have succeeded at least in bringing out a few of the aspects of this vast theme.

I dedicate this labour of mine to Dr. Giuseppe Antonelli as a mark of sincere friendship.

S. M.

Contents

Emperors		Writers
Second Century A.D.		
Marcus Aurelius 161–80		Dio Cassius 150–235
Commodus 180–92		Bardesanes 154–222
Septimius Severus 193–211		Montanus
		St. Hippolytus 165–235
Third Century	217–22 Callistus Pope	
Severus Alexander 222–35		St. Cyprian 200–58
Maximinus Thrax 235–38	236 Invasion of Alemanni and Franks	St. Dionysius of Alexandria 200–65
Philip the Arab 244–49	247 Invasion of Goths	Dexippus 210–70
Decius 249–51	251 Battle of Abrittus	Porphyry 233–304
Valerian 253–60		Commodian
Gallienus 260–8	Widespread barbarian invasions	Eusebius 260–340
		St. Methodius of Olympus d. 311
Diocletian 284–305	Reconstitution of imperial authority	Arnobius d. 330
Fourth Century		
Constantine 311–37	Christianity becomes official religion	Albericus
		St. Apollinarius 310–90
Constantius II 337–61		Themistius 317–90
Julian the Apostate 361–63		Ammianus Marcellinus 330–91
Jovian 363–64		St. Ambrose 339–97
Valens 364–78		St. Jerome 342–420
		Vegetius
Theodosius 379–95	Victory of Goths at Adrianople	St. John Chrysostom 347–407
395: division of the empire between Honorius (West) Arcadius (East)	396–408 Vandal Stilicho controls Western empire	St. Augustine 354–430
	398 Stilicho defeats rising of Gildo	Sulpicius Severus 363–425
		Sextus Aurelius Victor
		Claudian 370–404
		Synesius 370–414
Fifth Century		
	410 Alaric and Goths sack Rome	
	412 Ataulf leads Visigoths into Gaul	Zosimus
	419 Vallia establishes Visigothic Kingdom	Orosius
		Rutilius
Valentinian III rules in West 423–55	429 Genseric leads Vandals into Africa	Orientius
		Salvian 400–90
	451 Attila and Huns invade Gaul, defeated at Catalaunian Plains	Priscus
		Quodvultdeus Bp. of Carthage
Romulus Augustulus 475–6		Victor Bp. of Vita
End of Western empire 476		Cassiodorus 490–585
Odoacer King of Italy 476–89	480–547 St. Benedict of Nursia	
Theodoric King of Italy 489–526		
Sixth Century		
Amalasunta regent and Queen of Ostrogothic Italy 526–35		Procopius
Justinian 527–65	Partial temporary reconquest of Western empire	Jordanes
		Isidore of Seville 560–636
Totila King of Italy 541–55		
	590–604 Gregory the Great Pope	

The men and events included in this chart are generally those given prominence in this book. Many of the dates are approximate.

PART ONE

I

Two Ancient Ideas: Universal Empire and the Decadence of the State

The fall of the ancient world is not, of course, a completely unparalleled historical event. There have been other times when the human spirit has been crushed by the experience of decline, by the slow consumption or violent destruction of political organisms. The most interesting parallel may be found in the history of the very ancient East. The crisis with which this book is concerned, the crisis of the ancient world between the fifth and seventh centuries A.D., led from imperial Roman unity to fragmentation. Three thousand years earlier, in a region of enormous importance for the history of human civilization, lower Mesopotamia, a process which was in a sense opposite to this had led from the feudal separatism of the Sumerian states to the universal monarchy of the Semitic state of Akkad. The supranational Roman state dissolved between the fifth and seventh centuries A.D. About 2500–2300 B.C., in contrast, a large number of Sumerian cities entered into the dreadful last agony of decline just because they had never grasped the conception of a universal empire.

These events were widely separated in time, different and indeed even opposite in their structure; yet they were similar because in each case the new organisms germinated in a disrupted soil and the old structures collapsed under the weight of their own antiquity. No one could witness the great declines which took place in these two cases, and in others comparable with them, without a sensation of dread. The life of contemporaries, almost split into two, moved uneasily between the old and the new. In the presence of highly dramatic events of this kind, which overthrow ancient religious values, mankind has always wondered anxiously whether it might be possible in some way to hold off the final test. This is the origin of the idea of decadence, which coincides in one sense with that of collective guilt, 'the great sin'. But in the case of the end of the Roman Empire more is involved. Not only contemporary thought but also posterity has regarded this later crisis as the archetype of cultural decline and as a warning which also contains the key for the interpretation of the *whole* of our history. For this reason it may be interesting to make the comparison which is being suggested with the crisis of the Sumerian states which occurred three millennia earlier.

During the transition from the small, decadent, theocratic states of the Sumerians to the great universal state of Akkad, about 2500–2300 B.C., the Sumerians of Umma, under the leadership of Lugalzaggisi, attempted almost at the point of death to bring a universal state into existence. In fact this was to be achieved only by the Semites of Akkad somewhat later. A great contemporary, Urukagina, ruler of the Sumerian city of Lagash, had thought to offset the decadence of his state by reforms which represented a return to the original Sumerian institutions, and he had condemned the 'universalist' plans of the Sumerians of Umma. Urukagina offered a backward-looking interpretation of the crisis which was shaking the foundations of the old Sumerian world, once the creator of the highest cultural and artistic values. He thought that he had found the causes of decline in the greed of the governing classes, especially the priests. He claimed to have put an end to the injustices by reinstating the old arrangements, compelling the priests to give up their properties so that they might be restored to the god Ningirsu – that is, ultimately, to the state.

Urukagina, devoted to his god Ningirsu, denounced the ambitions and violations of the men of Umma. But the concept of a universal empire, which the Sumerians of Umma failed to turn into reality, became the great idea which the Near East realized over the millennia in various forms, from the state of Akkad (a little after Urukagina) to the empires of Assyria and Babylonia and finally the great Persian Empire, destroyed by Alexander the Great in 334–327 B.C. Alexander gave it to the West.

The Roman Empire was based on this idea. After its great Mediterranean conquests, Rome reconciled the ancient conception of the city state with the other conception, also as ancient as the state of Akkad, of a universal empire embracing both the city state and the 'nations' living within the empire. From Europe to Asia and Africa, the new state gave new life to the old cities. It created new cities, especially in Europe and Africa. The empire superimposed itself on the *nationes*, as in the East the great universal states, especially the Achaemenid, had superimposed themselves on the 'tongues' of the subject peoples. And so the crisis of the Sumerian world under Urukagina now appears in the memory of mankind as an episode which was rediscovered half a century ago, while the crisis of the Roman state has always seemed to be the yardstick for the understanding of world history, as the moment when the ancient forms gave way to the new. And indeed, with the consideration of the crisis of the ancient world, that is to say of the Roman world, the idea of decadence acquires an eternal meaning.

It contains the drama of the 'nations', which begin through troubles and convulsions to emerge from the collapsing framework of the great empire; the appearance of new peoples on the great stage of the classical world; the transition from a centralized and bureaucratic administration with a corresponding monetary economy to an economy which foreshadows feudalism in the West and seeks in the East to reconcile military service with peasant labour; the long decay of an agricultural system which attempted to strike a balance between the labour of slaves and of *coloni* bound to the soil. It is connected with the triumph of the Christian city of God, as conceived in the ideology of St. Augustine. This is in short the death of the ancient world, a death accompanied by the decline of values and social forms within and by the emergence of the Germans, Slavs and Arabs without.

The crisis of the Roman Empire has two other peculiarities which are closely connected with each other. Firstly, the end of antiquity was in a sense foreshadowed by the great upheavals which disturbed the Greek world from the time of the Peloponnesian War (431–404 B.C.) and still more in the fourth century B.C., the crisis which was grasped at its onset by the greatest historian of all time, Thucydides. Secondly, the crisis of Roman power was feared and, one might say, diagnosed, from the second century B.C., that is to say from the time of Rome's great Mediterranean conquests. With the knowledge we now have we can say that the idea of decadence spread in Italy as a result of the agrarian crisis which followed these conquests. Amongst the symptoms and consequences of the crisis in the second century B.C. and the early decades of the first century were the proletarianization of the Roman peasantry, the contraction of the areas cultivated by small proprietors,[1] the presence of 'imported and barbarian' manpower in regions like Etruria,[2] and the new agrarian legislation, with the resulting aspiration of the Italic peasantry to Roman citizenship.

The ancient Etruscan idea of 'ages', equivalent to about the lifetime of a man or rather more, provided a schematic framework for the expression of an awareness of the decline of certain traditional values. As early as *circa* 100 B.C. (according to some scholars even earlier, towards 200 B.C.) there was written in Etruria a page of the 'Vegoic' books, heavy with foreboding of guilt and decadence. 'When Jupiter took to himself the land of Etruria he intended that the fields and plots of land should be marked by boundary stones. ... But through the greed of the eighth age, the next and last to come,[3] men will criminally violate these marks, touching them and moving them. He who shall have touched them, however, and enlarged his own land and reduced another's shall be punished by the gods for this offence. If this shall happen through the fault of slaves, they shall have harder masters. If through the fault of the masters, the issue of the guilty man shall be destroyed, all his people shall die, shall be struck down by sicknesses and wounds and weakened in their limbs. The land shall be laid waste through storms and whirlwinds. Its produce will be beaten by rain and hail, dried up by heat and destroyed by blight. And there will be many dissensions among the people. Know then that this will happen if such crimes are com-

[1] See Tibiletti, *X Congresso di Scienze Storiche*, *Relazioni*, II (1955), pp. 235 ff.; Kousitchin, *Vestnik Drevnej istorii* (1957), I, pp. 64 ff.

[2] Mazzarino, *Historia* (1957), pp. 110 ff.

[3] On this translation see op. cit., p. 112.

mitted.' This Etruscan text has come down to us in a translation in vulgar Latin. It gave expression about 100 B.C., through a sacred voice, that of the 'nymph' Vegoia, to the idea of the decline of the Etruscan 'nation'. The Etruscans believed that their nation, or as they called it their 'name', had been allotted 'eight ages in all' (*gene* –'generations'–in Plutarch's Greek formulation), and the Vegoic text stated that the last of the eight ages, which was already near, would bring Etruscan history to an end in the midst of a ruined agriculture, through the fault of the 'crimes' of masters or slaves (Etruscan slaves were legally capable of owning property).

The idea of the decadence of the land whose produce no longer brings in enough was widespread in a different sense in other parts of Italy. Lucretius, living in the age of Cicero, gives us a picture of the peasant of his time made sorrowful by the cold resistance of the land to his efforts. The peasant's lament became for Lucretius a bitter statement of decadence as a materialistically determined fact: 'And now already our age is decayed (*fracta est aetas*). The earth grows weary and can scarce create small animals–earth that once created all the generations of men and gave birth to the gigantic bodies of beasts. . . . More than this, the same earth once created spontaneously for mortal men the golden corn and the joyful vines. It gave sweet fruits and happy pastures; and now on the contrary they will scarcely grow with all our labour. We exhaust our oxen and the farmer's strength and the ploughshare in the task, but the fields scarcely repay us, they are so greedy and demand so much labour. And now, shaking his head, the old ploughman sighs often, bewails his fruitless labour and compares the present time with times past, praising often the good fortune of his father. Sadly the planter of an aged and shrivelled vine blames the effect of time and wearies heaven, protesting that earlier men, full of piety, made an easy living out of narrow fields, although their plots of land were much smaller. He does not notice, with his laments, that everything slowly decays, marching towards the tomb, exhausted by the ancient lapse of time (*spatio aetatis defessa vetusto*).'[1] Not that Lucretius denied the possibility of progress, what he called the *experientia mentis pedetemptim progredientis*, the experience of the mind in its march towards progress. But decadence was a fact of

[1] Lucretius, II, 1150 ff.

nature for him–something which concerned nature and not the 'mind' of man. The process of becoming leads to what men call death–this is an old concept of Empedocles, and perhaps also of another fifth-century Greek philosopher Leucippus, which is coloured by bitterness in the Epicurean Lucretius.

Facts of human nature, however, demand a human explanation. The idea of decadence cannot be reduced to the exhaustion of the soil. It was the same Lucretius who said that men, driven by the false terror of death, spill the blood of their brothers in civil wars and that they hate and fear even the table of their kinsmen. His own time appeared to him to be ruled 'by the love of wealth and the blind longing for honours which lead wretched mortals to cross the boundaries of law and often to become accomplices and accessories of wrongs, striving night and day with immense labour to rise up to the heights of power'. His naturalistic determinism went with a consciousness of living 'in unhappy times for Rome', *patriae tempore iniquo*. This human drama, which the Epicurean Lucretius reduced to the false terror of death, was also an historical drama, even in a sense a consequence of the Roman conquests in the Mediterranean. In the eyes of contemporaries it appeared to be the presage not of a cosmic decadence, like the agricultural crisis in Lucretius, but a political and human crisis.

Amongst the contemporaries of Lucretius, Cicero gave it this political and human interpretation. As early as a century before this an alert consideration of the drama had disturbed thinkers and politicians in the circle of the Scipios. Here is another characteristic of the problem of the 'decadence of Rome': the supranational *imperium* of the Romans was already, many centuries before its fall, an object of anxiety on the part of those men who had contributed to its decisive establishment. In the second century B.C. Cornelius Scipio Nasica Corculum, consul in 155 B.C., made himself famous for opposing the point of view of Cato ('Carthage must be destroyed') and arguing that Carthage must be left standing, since its existence was necessary to prevent the decadence of the Roman state. Cornelius Scipio Aemilianus himself, the conqueror of Carthage, was affected by an obscure foreboding of the death of Rome in either the near or the distant future. Polybius, the great historian of Scipio's circle, was close to him at that time, in 146 B.C., and caught that moment of sadness in the great captain. 'He took my right arm,' he tells us, 'and he said to me: "Yes Polybius, that is good; but, I do not know why, I am afraid and have a foreboding that someone else will have to give the same news for our country" [as is now given for Carthage].' Polybius, as a Greek, did not regard Rome as his fatherland, but he had fallen in love with the lordly city with the enthusiasm of a man who knows that he is taking part in wonderful and great events. It was in this spirit that he, the 'pragmatic' historian, analysed the causes of the future 'fall' of Rome.[1]

'And it is also all too evident that ruin (*phthora*) and change are hanging over everything. The necessity of nature is enough to convince us of this. Now there are two ways in which any type of state may die. One is the ruin which comes from outside; the other, in contrast, is the internal crisis (*en autois*). The first is difficult to foresee, the second is determined from within. . . . When in fact a community has overcome many and serious dangers and has reached unquestioned power and lordship, new factors come into play. Prosperity takes its seat in that community and life turns towards luxury. Men become ambitious in their rivalries to achieve magistracies and other distinctions. As this goes on, the aspiration to magistracies, or the protest of those who see themselves rejected, the pride and the luxury, will give rise to decadence (*tes epi to keiron metaboles*). The masses of the people will be responsible for the crisis. They feel themselves abused by those who wish to pile up wealth; and by others, ambitious for office, they will be puffed up and flattered with demagogic wiles. Excited and stirred up, they will not wish to continue in obedience or to remain within the limits of law laid down by the patricians. They will want to have all the power, or the greatest power. After that the constitution will have the finest name there is: liberty and democracy. In reality, on the other hand, it will be the worst possible, the rule of the masses (*ochlokratia*).'

To this historian then, the future *phthora* of the Roman state seemed certain, and its causes exactly predictable as far as the

[1] See Mioni, *Polibio* (1949), pp. 49 ff.; Ryffel, *Μεταβολὴ πολιτειῶν* (1949), pp. 180 ff.; Ziegler, R. E., XXI, 2 (1952), pp. 1495 ff.; Sasso, *Rivista Storica Italiana* (1958), pp. 333 ff.

conflicts of classes within were concerned. He did not dare to make predictions openly about the 'external causes', what would be called 'the migrations of the people' five or six centuries after him. But in fact he had much to say on this question too. His view was not limited to Rome. The power of Rome's *imperium*, and even more its predictable end, were in his vision part of a general picture of the highly civilized states of the East, including not only those which had come to an end somewhat earlier but also others which would in their time fall under the blows of now distant barbarians. Polybius said that the empire of the Romans was infinitely superior to all the ancient universal empires.

'There was once a great empire of the Persians ..., [the Spartans] with difficulty held the hegemony over the Greeks for twelve years. ... The Macedonians ... having overthrown the Persians, added the empire of Asia to their dominion. Nevertheless, though they seemed to be lords of the vastest areas and of great power, they left the greater part of the world outside their government. ... But not so the Romans. They have subjected not just some parts of the world but almost the whole world; and thus they have left their empire invincible by those who live today and insuperable by those who are to come.'

Polybius was well enough acquainted with the Hellenistic states which Macedonian expansion had created in Asia. He was a personal friend of the Seleucid King Demetrius I. The Seleucid state, which had once extended from Syria to eastern Iran but was now in full decline, might have suggested to his historian's intelligence a confused image of what was in fact to be the crisis of the ancient world. It had been dismembered piece by piece. The Greek state of Bactria, consolidated in 206 B.C. by King Euthydemus, was separated from it. Finally in 130 B.C. nomadic horsemen originating in central Asia had overthrown and 'barbarized' Greek Bactria, the vital outpost of the Hellenistic world. Polybius used this very word, 'barbarized'. He was reflecting on these recent events of 130 B.C., which struck a world that was far distant from the Roman Empire in space but, like the Roman empire, an expression of classical culture. The invasions of the barbarians into the ancient world were thus first heralded in eastern Iran six centuries before the formation of the Romano-barbarian kingdoms in the west. Polybius at least partly understood the terrifying lesson, and in a disturbed and significant passage[1] he put into the mouth of Euthydemus, the creator of Bactrian power, a reasoned forecast of the 'migration of peoples' into the highly civilized states.

'The title and dignity of a king belonged to him [independently of the Seleucid state]. If Antiochus did not agree, neither would be sure of his power. [That is to say that barbarization menaced both states.] There were in fact considerable forces of nomads and both of them–Antiochus and Euthydemus–ran the risk of irruption into their states. If they admitted the invaders, the country would be, without any doubt, barbarized. . . . Antiochus [III, the Great] understood the importance of the aforesaid reasons and accepted Euthydemus's proposal.'

Let us sum up. In Polybius's *Histories* we already find the two themes which are going to be dominant in the interpretation of the end of the ancient world, even down to the present day. On the one hand there is the 'internal' explanation which is already applied by Polybius to the constitutional structure of the Roman Empire with the deduction of its future fall from the impossibility of overcoming class conflicts. On the other hand there is the 'external' explanation which Polybius applies to the 'barbarization' of the Greco-Bactrian state in which a great structure of classical culture, mingled with Iranian, was submerged under the flood of Iranian nomads, impelled in their turn by the wave of Huns, enclosed in their chivalric iron armour and attracted towards the Bactrian state in the same way as the Goths, five or six centuries later, were attracted towards the Roman Empire.

In Polybius's thought, reflection on the greatness and decadence of Rome is flanked by the two opposed interpretations of the ancient crisis, the 'internal' and the 'external'. In the period which followed the time of Polybius the theme of 'internal' decadence was touched on in various ways. The Etruscan Vegoic text, as we saw, spoke in a tone of religious emotion about Etruria rather than Rome. Agricultural conditions differed widely at that time between the different parts of the peninsula–for example the great estate was the rule amongst the Etruscans, but small properties amongst the Marsi, and therefore the first were hostile and the second favourable to Livius

[1] Polybius, XI, 34.

Drusus.[1] The civil wars of the first century B.C. and the War of Spartacus (73–71 B.C.), however, revealed the Italian agricultural crisis. In spite of his thesis that decadence was a natural occurrence due to the exhaustion of the soil, Lucretius did not forget the human aspect and the great problems which disturbed Roman life as a result of the conquests. In this respect he spoke, as an Epicurean, not of 'decadence' but of the 'false terror of death'. In contrast to Polybius the emphasis in his outlook did not fall upon the rebellion of the masses. The 'terror of death' was something that existed in the inner conscience of unsatisfied ambition.

Cicero saw the idea of the decadence of Rome in two forms: the decay of manners and the lack of really great men (*virorum penuria*). 'Before our times the customs of our people produced outstanding individuals and ancient customs and traditional institutions were preserved by eminent personalities. In our age, however, the state has come to be like a painting which is remarkable but already fading because of old age, and people neglect not only to restore the

[1] The tribunate of Livius Drusus in 91 B.C. is of great importance for the understanding of Roman history. By distributing lands in Italy to Roman citizens Livius Drusus struck at the interests of the great landed proprietors who were masters of slaves, but he benefited the small peasants of Italy to whom he promised Roman citizenship so that they too might participate in the distribution of land (on this see Bernardi, *Nuova Rivista Storica* (1944–5), pp. 60 ff. and, rather differently, Gabba, *Athenaeum* (1954), pp. 41 ff.) or at least would not be damaged by it. Faced by the possibilities which Drusus opened to them the agriculturalists of Italy reacted in two opposite ways. The Marsi, the Samnites and the Lucani–especially the first of these–were with him. They saw in the acquisition of Roman citizenship, amongst other things, a sure way to defend their small properties or to participate in the near future in colonial projects. The Etruscan peasants, on the other hand–a good many of whom were *lautni* of foreign origin, Egyptian for instance (*Historia* (1957), pp. 110 ff.)–were for the most part hostile to Drusus because of their devotion to their owners of large estates. To sum up, the Etruscan-Umbrian big estate was opposed to the small landed property of the Marsi, Samnites and Lucani. This distinction in Italian agriculture in the first century B.C. may have left traces down to the late empire. According to some scholars Southern Italy was the region par excellence for *exploitation de peu d'étendue*, that is the opposite of Northern Italy (Déléage, *La Capitation du Bas-Empire* (1945), pp. 219 ff., where however *Cod. Th.* XI, 12, 1, is made to refer to Italy rather than Gaul and also the difference between the designations *ingum* and *millena* does not seem to me to imply a difference in extent). In any case a certain continuity in Italian agriculture may be established in some areas for the whole imperial period. E.g. the wines of Cesena were equally sought after in the first century A.D. and the fourth century A.D. (*Cod. Th.* XI, 1, 6). There was a break in the Middle Ages with the Lombard system of proprietary churches which struck at the Tuscan estates. (One may note however that in the late Empire *Tuscia et Umbria* was normally regarded as belonging to the vicariate of Rome; it was 'Southern Italy'.)

original colours in it, but even to preserve its shape and outlines.'[1] An opponent of Cicero, Sallust, in his anxious analysis,[2] also turned his attention to the ruling groups and their dreams of wealth and office. For him decadence was inseparable from the disappearance of *virtus*–a theme which will recur in Machiavelli. According to Sallust therefore the crisis of social customs and the coming of *luxuria* have a clear political consequence which was placed roughly, as later by another historian Velleius, in 146 B.C. This was also the teaching of the first-century Stoic philosopher Posidonius (Calpurnius Piso, on the other hand, put the beginning of moral decay in 154 B.C. and Livy later took it back to 188 B.C.). It was accompanied in Sallust by a passionate involvement in the question which was almost polemical. It was in this period that the word 'decline' in the sense of 'decline of the state' was first used in the Roman world. *Inclinata res publica* is a phrase which both Cicero and Sallust used. Sallust's vision of decadence has a basis of general sadness. The formula 'everything that is born must die' (*omnia orta intereunt*) occurs at least twice in his writings. Apart from this his foreboding of the end of Rome shows him rather less resigned than Polybius. He did not abandon hope; quite the reverse. He wrote to Caesar:

'This is my opinion. Since everything that is born dies, when the fate of death comes to the city of Rome, citizens will fight with citizens and then, weary and exhausted, they will be the prey of some king or nation. Otherwise, neither the whole world nor all the peoples together have the power to abase or to harm this empire. We must then consolidate the benefits of concord and destroy the evils of discord.'

The theory that the end of the ancient world will be due only to civil wars to some extent puts off the great fear. A superior man can restore concord. It is true that the return of civil war after the death of Caesar brought back the feeling of despair in many circles. In the sixteenth epode Horace spoke, if we translate his words into Polybian terms, of 'internal ruin' (*suis et ipsa Roma viribus ruit*) and 'external ruin' (*barbarus heu cineres insistet victor et urbem eques sonante verberabit ungula*). But the hope of a man who would put an

[1] Cicero, *De Re Publica*, V, 1, 2.

[2] See Steidle, 'Sallusts Historische Monographien', *Historia*, Einzelschriften, Heft 3 (1958).

end to civil wars allayed the anxieties of many. It had been Sallust's hope, and a modern Italian historian (Aldo Ferrabino) has said therefore that 'Rome, the Rome which Sallust envisages, does not have its end in decadence.'

The prospect of an inevitable end was also abandoned on the religious plane. In Etruria the old prophecies which regarded the eighth 'age' as the last and placed its beginning in the year 88 B.C. were relinquished. The soothsayer Volcacius added the ninth and tenth 'ages' and thus altered the whole traditional Etruscan calculation. But, especially for Rome, the optimism of the auguries had a profound significance. Faith in life triumphed over the great fear of imminent death. In the age of Varro (116–27 B.C.) a certain Vettius had drawn attention to the prophetic significance of the twelve vultures seen by Romulus for, as he said, Rome had at that time passed through the first 120 years from its foundation and therefore was destined to last not twelve decades but twelve centuries, 1200 years. According to Varro's prophet friend, the death of Rome would be placed roughly in what was to be the time of Attila the Hun.

Astrology suggested yet more speculations. The idea of a more or less inevitable and predestined 'decadence' was replaced by the idea of a 'new foundation' of Rome with fixed cycles. As a result of the introduction of the Julian calendar with 365 days, there was a theory of great cycles of 365 years, after which communities would suffer either death or renewal. In the year 365 from its foundation, Rome had survived the threat of death–the burning by the Gauls–through the intervention of Camillus, a new Romulus. It was therefore deduced that now, at the end of a new cycle of 365 years starting from Camillus, Rome had found its 'new Romulus' in Augustus, who was honoured with the tribunician power in 23 B.C.[1]

Julius Caesar and his 'son' Augustus had in fact overcome the age of the civil wars. After them, through the foundation of the Augustan

[1] I would explain with this hypothesis Livy's *trecentesimus sexagesimus quintus annus agitur* in the famous speech of Camillus to which Hubaux especially has drawn attention. In the explanation which I propose, Livy would obtain the idea from Augustan circles. This overcomes the objection, which was always stated against Hubaux, that a 'great year' of 365 years was impossible before the Julian calendar. Cf. Hubaux, *Rome et Véies* (1958).

state in 27 and 23 B.C. the Polybian problem of the decadence of Rome had to be stated in different terms. The Roman empire was to endure another five centuries in the west–in some parts of the west, seven, eight or even ten centuries if it was regarded as continuing in its medieval Roman or Byzantine form. In the east, in the form of the Byzantine empire, it was to have its great crisis in the seventh century and then to continue, after the loss of some important territories, down to the establishment of the Latin empire in 1204 and, after the Latin interregnum, down to 1453. This was a perspective which stretched an immense distance into the future. Still, from the first centuries of the empire founded by Augustus, men continued to state Polybius's problem. In short the problem of the death of Rome was raised before Rome died.

The ideal categories of the problem were now displaced both in space and in time. In space because Rome was no longer confined to the old city, or even to Italy. Its provinces were dotted with its colonies and from the time of Trajan (A.D. 98–117) it would be possible to have Roman emperors born outside Italy. From the year 212 all freemen in the provinces, except the *dediticii*,[1] obtained Roman citizenship. In time because now the problem of the 'rebellion of the masses', which Polybius had stated, could not be confined to the proletarian masses of Rome, which he had had in mind. It was extended to the whole of Italy and beyond, it came to include the peasant masses of Syria, Illyricum, the Celtic provinces, Africa and Egypt, in short the 'nations' (*ethne*) which inhabited all the

[1] On this constitution granted by the Emperor Caracalla in 212 see below, ch. 11. We do not however know precisely who were the *dediticii* whom Caracalla excluded from the benefits of citizenship. In terms of pure law all those inhabitants of the empire who were not bound to Rome by a treaty of alliance (*foedus*) were called *dediticii*, but in 212 the word certainly had a more limited meaning. According to some scholars, including the author of this book, they could still include considerable peasant masses, for example in Egypt, who were not assimilated to Greco-Roman culture. According to others the name referred only to barbarians received into the empire in relatively recent times. (Another category of *dediticii* was composed of manumitted slaves who, because of previous crimes, could not become Roman or Latin citizens.) The formula used by Caracalla which has come down to us runs (P.Giessen 40): 'I therefore grant the citizenship of the Romans to all, [the foreign peoples of] the world, [this grant] relating to . . . excepting the *dediticii*.' The various interpretations proposed always assume an intransitive [*M*]ένοτος. I understand it as transitive and therefore translate it as 'relating to'. Recent literature and discussion in D'Ors, *Emerita* (1956), p. 10; Oliver, *American Journal of Philology* (1955), p. 297.

provinces of this immense empire. No longer, as in the age of the civil wars, was the crisis of the ruling class confined to the discontent of the Roman or Italian proletariat. At the end of the ancient world the universal Roman empire would have to take account of the problem of the fanatical masses of Donatist Africa, of Nestorian Syria, of monophysite Egypt, added to the hostility of incompletely romanized Celtic and Pannonian peasants bound to the soil by cruel fetters. This then was the problem of the nations. There was also the problem of the threat of 'barbarization' which Polybius had distinguished in distant Bactria. Now, through the passage of time, the problem of the 'external causes' of decadence was maturing for Rome too as Polybius had said.

The foreboding of a 'scientifically' predictable end as it is found in Polybius–or, understood in ethical terms, as it is found in Cicero and Sallust–established even in the culture of republican Rome a very close connection between the idea of decadence and that of the predictability of historical events. For this reason the Polybian 'prophecy' was most completely in tune with contemporary thought in another period in which men believed in the power of foreseeing the destined course of history, the age of romanticism. A century ago in 1858 there appeared a book by Lasaulx called *The Human Power of Prophecy in Poets and Thinkers*. It was a completely romantic book from beginning to end and today it is justly forgotten. In its day it was remarkably successful because the thesis of the 'predictability of history' which it maintained had tenacious supporters and also very powerful opponents, the chief of whom was Gervinus. It was natural that Polybius should be Lasaulx's chief exhibit for, if the historian of the republican period had been able to foresee the crisis of the Roman state, all the other 'prophecies', such as that of Nicholas Cusanus about the revolution against the German princes or that of Leibnitz about the great revolution 'bred by criticism', acquired legitimate places in the history of the human spirit. At the bottom of the romantic hypothesis about the 'predictability' of history, however, was above all the Hegelian doctrine of satisfied ages and of pacifying old age. The Polybius of the romantics was therefore somewhat far removed from the real Polybius, who rather preferred facts to patterns. But the age of Polybius and Sallust and the romanticism of a century ago had in common the gloomy sense of a connection between the notion of decadence and the predictability of history.

In this sense Polybius stands at the crisis of the Roman republic in the same way that Burckhardt and Nietzsche stand at the crisis of our time. In both cases we have men who suppose themselves to be living at a mature period (the foundation of the greatest empire in the world for Polybius; the culture of the nineteenth century for Burckhardt and Nietzsche) but also think that they can perceive dense shadows in the future course of events. They are under the illusion that their pessimism has a 'scientific' justification. In fact they are forcing the facts into a Procrustean bed made of certain presuppositions. The myth of progressive decadence, as it is expressed at the dawn of classical civilization in Hesiod's idea of progressive movement away from the golden age, has an unmistakably religious origin in the idea of 'eternal recurrence' which has been studied by Mircea Eliade in a famous book. A similar attitude expressed in a cyclical form leads to the idea of *saecula* ('centuries') which are born and die. As we have seen, it gave rise in ancient Italy to the Vegoic teaching which placed the end of the Etruscan nation in the eighth *saeculum* and interpreted it as a punishment by the god Tinia (Jupiter). There was also another possible attitude which men could take in confronting their historical position, to believe that decadence might be overcome through a return to the old order of things. This was the formula of Urukagina as early as the third millennium B.C. It may be compared with the teaching of Sallust, according to which one 'must consolidate the benefits of concord' in order to hold off the death of Rome; and also the 'new foundation' by Camillus and Augustus comes into the same picture. Lucretius's naturalistic interpretation, according to which decadence resolved itself into soil-exhaustion, moved the problem on to a biological and cosmic plane. Cicero's image of the decadent Roman state as an old and fading picture put the idea of old age back on an ethico-political plane. Cicero insisted on the *virorum peniuria*. In the ancient, as in the modern, world the idea of decadence involved the most diverse perspectives.

2

The End of Time or the Crisis of an Empire?

When the political structure had been transformed with the coming of Augustus the great fears disappeared. Rome and Italy had been saved and the provinces reorganized in a definitive manner. Very many people in the generation which enjoyed this renaissance, the second Augustan generation, no longer wished to hear about decadence of manners or other such old delusions. The poet Ovid belonged to this generation, and the ancient protests of the 'ruminatores' like Varro irritated him. What were the claims of these admirers of past time, these merciless critics of luxury and *avaritia*? 'Other men,' said Ovid, 'like past times, but I am happy to be born now; this age suits my way of life.' Far from speaking of decadence he liked to speak of progress in technology (mining, commerce) and culture. 'Today there is good taste (*cultus*); and our age flees from that *rusticitas* which used to be found amongst our ancestors.'[1]

But some old problems were still unsolved, especially economic problems. The decline of Italian agriculture repeatedly made itself felt. It had been hard hit in the age of the civil wars and ruined, as early as the time of Spartacus, by the plantation system. Financial crises revealed obvious difficulties. If at the time of Sulla the poet Lucretius had bewailed the exhaustion of the land, a remedy was

[1] Ovid, *Ars Amatoria*, III, 121 ff.: a real exaltation of progress.

now sought in the wisdom of men. In the second half of the first century A.D. a famous writer on agriculture, Columella, returned to the lament over the decadence of Italian agronomy. He praised ancient times, that old complaint which Ovid had found unbearable.

There was another problem for which the optimism of men like Ovid found no easy remedy. The establishment of the principate initiated a monarchical régime based on the *auctoritas* of the *princeps*. The ruling class witnessed the dissolution of the ancient tradition of republican liberty, and this was a bitter blow, especially in the early days. Grief-stricken regret for ancient liberty, connected with the idea that the new monarchical régime is a sign of old age, pervades the bitter pages of Seneca the Elder, who was born in the republican period but died during the reign of Caligula. In the depths of his grief the hopeless old man dreamed of ancient republican Rome and re-created the tragic events of the civil wars.

'The first infancy of Rome was under Romulus, its founder and, as it were, nourisher. Then the city went through boyhood under the other kings. As it approached manhood it ceased to tolerate servitude and, throwing off the yoke, preferred to obey laws rather than kings. This adolescence finished with the end of the Punic Wars. Then Rome's power was strengthened and its youth began. In fact, having swept aside Carthage, which had long contested the first place, Rome extended its power over the whole world, by land and by sea, until, having subjugated all the kings and nations, and having no more objects in war, it misused its own power and so exhausted itself. This was its first old age, when, torn by the civil wars and weakened by an internal crisis, it fell again under monarchical rule as if in a second childhood. In fact, having lost the liberty which it had defended under the leadership and by the initiative of Brutus, it grew so old that it seemed not to have the power to sustain itself without resting on the support of the monarchs.'

One can detect in this biological analysis of the history of Rome[1] a return to the Ciceronian idea of the Roman state as a 'picture fading because of old age', but in a writer of the time of Caligula the idea of the decadence of old age is at once a cry of grief and an

[1] On this passage in Seneca see Hartke, *Römische Kinderkaiser* (1950), pp. 393 ff. The idea of the old age of Rome is then found in Florus; cf. P. Zancan, *Floro e Livio* (1942), pp. 13–20 (fundamental for the history of the idea of decadence in this period). In general cf. Pöschl, *Gymnasium* (1956), pp. 190 ff.

exaltation of liberty, of liberty seen as the time of youth. We shall have to remember Seneca when we come to deal with humanistic thought, according to which Rome's *inclinatio* was the result of the imperial régime, and even when we examine Seeck's idea of the 'elimination of the best men'.[1]

It is no accident that the use of the word 'decline' (*inclinare*) in questions of manners and literature begins in the first and second centuries, especially among the same governing classes of the empire. We find in Pliny *inclinatis iam moribus* and in Quintilian *inclinasse eloquentiam.* Thus there is a transference of the idea of decline, which is applied to the state in Cicero, to the sphere of culture. This is the age in which there is talk of the decadence of the arts in Petronius and of eloquence in Tacitus and Quintilian. Roman tradition, represented by the senatorial classes and by high culture, has then worked out its own kind of humanism. This same concept of *inclinatio* will be, in modern history, the great discovery of our Quattrocento. Juvenal takes up again Varro's old theme of *luxuria* as the source of evils: 'worse than arms, *luxuria* oppresses us and takes revenge for the world which we conquered; since Romans ceased to be poor there is no crime which is not committed among us.'

Outside the traditional world, which expressed itself wonderfully in the Senecan idea of monarchical old age, a great spiritual revolution was giving a new sense of tragedy to the crisis poisoning the classical world: the Christian revolution. In certain of its manifestations it may be compared with some contemporary expressions of the Judaic world, humiliated and overthrown by the Roman conquest and by the oppression which followed. There is, for instance, the *Commentary on Habbakuk*, one of the texts revealed to us by the Dead Sea discoveries, in which the spiritual drama of Judaism is declared and the blame for it given to an impious priest, described by the Commentary as 'he who, because of the insult offered to the Master of Justice and the members of his community, was given by God into the hands of his enemies that they might ruin him with an act of destruction, with bitterness for his soul,

[1] In modern terminology one might say that for Seneca the Elder history is 'the history of liberty'. In contrast to the ancients, modern interpreters of history as the history of liberty often take refuge in biological formulations. One thinks of Croce and Rüstow.

since he had acted in an impious manner towards his chosen'. This 'impious priest' is condemned by the *Commentary on Habbakuk* together with all those 'who were silent when the Master of Justice was punished and have not helped him against the man of falsehood who offended against the Law'. The *Commentary* adds to the condemnation of the 'impious priest' and the 'man of falsehood' an implacable hatred of the Romans (*kittim*) who 'will sacrifice to their banners, and their instruments of war will be worshipped by them'.

Here the idea of religious guilt replaces the idea of decadence, and the Romans, together with those Jews who were traitors, are the hated authors of the offence to God. Primitive Christianity, more tolerant than this towards the Roman Empire but still formed in the same atmosphere of the Jewish spiritual revival, reveals, amongst other things, one very serious aspect of the crisis of the ancient world, namely the social oppression which characterized Roman rule over the peasants of the provinces. St. James, who like Jesus was condemned to death in the end, expressed at the very beginning of the empire this interpretation of the world crisis, seen from the tormented point of view of the Judaic-Palestinian world where there were powerful stirrings of those ideas which would one day make the classical world collapse upon itself.

'Next a word to you who have great possessions. Weep and wail over the miserable fate descending on you. Your riches have rotted; your fine clothes are moth-eaten; your silver and gold have rusted away, and their very rust will be evidence against you and consume your flesh like fire. You have piled up wealth in an age that is near its close. The wages you never paid to the men who mowed your fields are loud against you, and the outcry of the reapers has reached the ears of the Lord of Hosts. You have lived on earth in wanton luxury, fattening yourselves like cattle–and the day for slaughter has come. You have condemned the innocent and murdered him; he offers no resistance.'[1]

A few Roman knights, 'men with gold rings', as St. James himself calls them, were carried away beside the Palestinian peasants in these earliest synagogues of the Christians. Both listened to the dramatic prophecy of St. James on the end of a world ruled by

[1] From the New English Bible, St. James's Epistle.

privilege. We can perhaps imagine the gloomy looks of the Roman knights, and the eagerness for liberation of the Palestinian peasants around whom the rule of the privileged had erected a kind of invisible prison. Soon the new faith won over great masses of adherents, and the idea of the imminent end of the Roman empire must have dominated the minds of many in that great mass of Christians who were burnt like torches and cruelly martyred in Nero's Rome. Besides, the idea of the end of Rome was for them identical with the idea of the end of the world. Antichrist would come and the breath of the Lord would destroy him. With the passage of time, since the end of the world no longer appeared imminent (and even St. Paul's injunctions had assumed its continuance) the attitudes of the Christians to the imperial crisis began to diverge somewhat. Some, exalting the work of Providence, trustingly reconciled the empire of Rome with Christianity; others disparaged the empire and tried to explain its imminent fall to themselves, with disguised pleasure, by the coming of Antichrist, Nero reborn, who would be smashed by the blast of the Lord.

Two sacred texts at any rate inspired their expectation. One was the Book of Daniel, written between 167 and 165 B.C. This book, which is also cited by Jesus in St. Matthew's Gospel, seemed to declare that four monarchies succeed each other in history, all rulers of the world. They are represented by the parts of the statue dreamt of by Nebuchadnezzar, respectively by the head of gold, the breast and arms of silver, the belly of copper and the legs of iron, the toes and feet of the statue being of iron mixed with clay. Furthermore, the vision of Daniel included four beasts which also came to be interpreted as the four monarchies. The end of the world was to follow immediately after the disappearance of the last monarchy; this was the point on which fears and hopes were concentrated.

The other great book, the Revelation of St. John, envisaged the serpent giving its strength to a beast which climbed out of the sea with seven heads and ten horns, ruler of every tribe, people, language, nation, worshipped by all the inhabitants of the earth. It saw an angel pointing to an abominable woman 'the great city which has government over the kings on earth' and another announcing the end of the 'great city, the powerful Babylon' on whose death the merchants weep. Many interpreters saw in this apocalyptic symbolism an announcement of the end of the world, the fall of Rome the greatest of the cities. About a century after St. John, towards the end of the reign of the emperor Marcus Aurelius (d. A.D. 180), a Christian oracular poet imagined the 'Antichristian' decline of Rome, marked by impiousness and tribulation, arising out of the oppression which burdened the provincials and filled the houses of the emperor with riches. In this poet the end of the Roman world is a religious certainty, not an excited foreboding; the apocalytic images are mingled with a vision of imminent famine and civil war. He detests the universality of an empire in which, as if in a huge crucible, many nations are ground into a single colour. Therefore his evocation, flashing with hatred, is not so much an examination of the causes which will lead to the death of the empire but rather a curse uttered in burning eagerness to invoke the shattering of an unjust state. Fundamentally, for this oracular poet, the Roman Caesar is the enemy of the provincials. The idea of the oppressed nations which had appeared tentatively even in the writings of the Augustan age acquired, with the luminous power of the new faith, a great moral force and was combined with the certainty of the decadence and the imminent end of Rome.

'An old monarch [Marcus Aurelius] will have a long period of rule. He will be a wretched king who will shut up all the treasures of the world in his houses so that when the fugitive matricide [Antichrist, Nero reborn] comes from the end of the earth, they shall be distributed and shall be a great wealth for Asia. Then you will weep, O proud Queen, scion of Latin Rome; giving up the senatorial tunic of the rulers you will put on mourning clothes. There will be no more glory for your pride, nor, unhappy creature, will you find any comfort, but will be subdued. And indeed the glory of the eagle-bearing legions will end. Where then will be your strength? What land, unjustly enslaved by your follies, will help you? Great confusion will come among all the men of the earth then, when the Almighty, appearing on the Throne, will judge the souls of the living and dead and the whole world. Then neither will parents be dear to their children nor children to their parents, because of the impiousness and desperate tribulation. Gnashing of teeth and separation and imprisonment will follow when the cities fall and the earth opens. And when the red dragon comes on the waves with his belly full to afflict your children, and famine comes and civil war, then will be the end of the world and the last day and for the glorious who are called the judgment of immortal God. There will be pitiless anger in the first place against the Romans, a time thirsty for blood and an unhappy life.

'Evil for you, land of Italy, great barbarian race: you did not know whence you had come, naked and unworthy, into the light of the sun, to plunge again naked into this same place and at last to come to the Judge since you yourself judge unjustly. . . . Gigantic hands will make you fall alone, through the world, down from your height and you will lie under the earth. You will disappear burnt by oil and pitch and sulphur and much smoke and you will be dust for centuries. And whoever looks will hear from Hades the great wail of grief and the grinding of teeth and you beating your godless breast with your hand. . . .

'Because the empire of Rome, once flourishing, the ancient lord of the cities around, has vanished. The blooming land of Rome shall conquer no more when the conqueror [Antichrist] comes from Asia with Ares. When he has finished all that he will come upon the City which is puffed up. [O Rome] you will be 948 years old when the fate of death will descend with force upon you, completing the years of your name.'

This Christian oracular writer presented the end of the ancient world (and that meant of the world) as imminent. He placed it 948 years after the foundation of Rome, that is to say in A.D. 195. But in this case again the eager apocalyptic expectation went unfulfilled. Marcus Aurelius, under whom this was written, was succeeded by Commodus, a young monarch whose personality was full of contradictions. He was extremely handsome and yet sick with a malady of old age, proud of presenting himself as the 'Roman Hercules' who could slay beasts and fight like a gladiator but in love with Marcia, a Christian woman to whom he had given almost all the honours of an empress. In his time the idea of the end of the world once again receded; he was a peaceful emperor and put an end to the wars undertaken by his father Marcus against the barbarians who threatened the frontiers from without. But the idea of the decadence of the empire did not recede. The old governing classes, pagan and admirers of Marcus, said that an age of iron had appeared with the coming of Commodus. For them the good period had ended with Marcus. Dio Cassius, a historian who was a senator in this period, said '[after the death of Marcus] history passed from an empire of gold to one of iron, rusted'. Herodian, another historian, and perhaps an imperial freedman, who lived at Rome in this period, also thought that with the death of Marcus Aurelius an epoch of decadence began.

'If one considers the period from Augustus onwards, from the time when the empire of the Romans took on a monarchical form, one will not find in all the years, amounting to about two centuries, up to Marcus, such rapid successions of reigns or such varied fortunes in civil and foreign wars or movements of peoples and occupations of cities in our empire and beyond, or earthquakes or atmospheric disturbances, or abnormal behaviour by usurpers and emperors. For previously there is either no record at all or only rarely of such things.'

The decadence of the ancient world appeared to the two pagans, Dio Cassius and Herodian, in terms quite opposed to those formulated at the end of the reign of Marcus by the Christian oracular poet. For him the death of Rome coincided with the reign of Marcus, but for the two pagans the reign of Marcus was the state's last golden age. In the oracular vision the end of Rome was the just sentence for tributary oppression and the wars of Marcus. In Herodian's interpretation, on the contrary, the great crisis began at the moment when Commodus, the peaceful emperor, had preferred the delights of Rome to the war and the icy Danube, and his preference for Rome had been inspired by his 'abnormal' and 'paradoxical' life, to use Herodian's Greek phrases.

The reign of Commodus was followed by the year of the five emperors (193), the civil war and the reigns of the Severi. Amongst many Christians the great hope remained alive and Montanus believed that the collapse of this world was imminent. In Pontus Christian peasants left their fields, sold their goods and awaited the day of judgment, while the same expectation of the imminent end led men, women and children in Syria to move to meet the Kingdom of God in the desert. Tertullian prayed 'that the end might be delayed', *pro mora finis*. And here a great Christian writer, St.

Hippolytus, intervenes. He too starts, in his investigation of the end of the world, from the Book of Daniel and the Revelation of St. John. In his *Commentary on Daniel* St. Hippolytus gave an unforgettable expression to this end of the world which coincides with the end of the Roman empire. He places it in A.D. 500, near to the date earlier predicted by the pagan Vettius who had, we may remember, allowed Rome twelve centuries of life. But the difference between Vettius, the pagan of the age of Varro, and St. Hippolytus, the Christian of the age of Severus, is enormous. St. Hippolytus attributes the end of Rome to the rise of the democracies.

'The toes [of the statue in the dream of Nebuchadnezzar] are meant to represent the democracies which are to come and which will be separate one from another like the ten toes of the statue on which iron will be mingled with clay.'

These 'democracies' arise from the 'nations', 'while ten kings', Hippolytus says elsewhere, 'will partition the empire according to the nations'. Hippolytus has seen correctly the time and manner of the death of Rome, for the end of the ancient world was in effect to a large extent a victory of the parts over the whole, of the periphery over the weakened centre. The apocalyptic perspective drew Hippolytus's attention towards the internal contradictions and the final destiny of the empire of the world. Apart from that, the problem of the 'nations', the 'democracies', which would one day divide the empire of Rome between themselves, constantly dominated Hippolytus's thought. 'The *Kyrios* [Lord] was born in the forty-second year of Augustus, with whom the flowering of the Roman empire began. Through the Apostles he called all the nations and all the tongues and made them into one nation of Christian faithful who bore the name of the *Kyrios*, the new name, in their hearts. The empire which rules us according to the power of Satan wished to imitate all this and so it too gathered together the strongest from all the nations and armed them for war, calling them by the name of Romans.'

This view emphasized one aspect of the crisis, the condition of the peoples within the universal state of Rome. Another Christian writer later examined the crisis in moral life, a more general aspect but an equally interesting one; a Sallustian theme dropped into the dramatic atmosphere of the third century A.D. He was a distinguished Carthaginian rhetorician, Cyprian. Within the officially pagan empire the Christians were not a sparse minority but a noteworthy section of the population, strengthened by their faith. Under Commodus the emperor's concubine herself, Marcia, had been a Christian;[1] half a century later the Christian communities were still stronger and even one emperor, Philip the Arab, who ruled from 244 to 249, was regarded as a Christian.

Cyprian was converted to Christianity at the time of Philip the Arab. The fury of war had taken hold of the empire under Philip's predecessor. The new emperor, Christian or near to the Christians, had arranged a peace, but this was not enough to quieten the anguished soul of Cyprian. The eager neophyte thought he could see in the everyday life of Roman society an inexorable decline of values equivalent to a sentence of death. He protested against the wars. 'If someone commits murder he regards it as a crime; if the murder is carried out in the name of the state, it is considered virtuous.' In the administration of justice again he saw the hopes of a better society vanishing. 'The laws are written on the twelve tables and in the public edicts but the judge sells his decision to the highest bidder'; wills are falsified; 'law is in league with crime'. In 251 the tragedy deepened. Decius, a pagan emperor, had been ruling since 249. The fifty-year-old Cyprian returned to his battle. In his letter addressed to Demetrianus he tried to reaffirm his conception of the inexorable decadence of an aged world against pagans who attributed the ills of the state to the new faith. This was, as we have already seen, a Lucretian motif, but Cyprian made it his own and felt on all sides the tiredness of old age and the cold touch of death.

'You ought to know that this world has already grown old. It no longer has the powers which once supported it; the vigour and strength by which it was once sustained. Even if we Christians did not speak and give expression to the warnings of the Holy Scriptures and the divine prophecies, the world itself is already announcing its decay and the events themselves are the evidence of its decline and fall. In winter there is no longer plenty of water for the seed, in summer no longer the accustomed heat to mature them; nor

[1] Or at least very close to the Christians. Bishop Hippolytus who expresses the most unyielding Christianity calls her *philotheos*, 'pious'. She was devoted to the Bishop of Rome, Victor. Cf. ch. 7, below.

is the spring weather happy nor autumn fertile in produce. The production of silver and gold has gone down in the exhausted mines as well as the production of marble; the worked-out veins give less and less from day to day. The cultivator is no longer in the fields, the sailor on the seas, soldier in the barracks, honesty in the market-place, justice in the law court, solidarity in friendship, skill in the arts, discipline in manners. Do you really think that so aged a world can have the energy that youth, still fresh and new, could once find? Everything which approaches its end and turns towards decline and death must necessarily lose vigour. As in its own setting the sun sends out rays less bright and fiery, so also the moon is less bright in its waning, and the tree which had once been fertile and green, its branches drying up, becomes sterile and deformed by old age. . . .

'You blame the Christians because everything is reduced with the ageing of the world. But it is certainly not the Christians' fault that old men lose their strength and no longer have the powers of hearing they once had or their speed or sight, their sturdiness, hardiness or health. Once the long-lived attained 800 or 900 years, now with difficulty a hundred. We see bald children, the hair disappearing before growing; nowadays life does not end but *begins* with old age. . . .

'As for the greater frequency of wars, the more serious preoccupation with overcoming famines and sterility, the raging of sicknesses which ruin health, the devastation wreaked by the plague in the midst of men–this too, make no mistake, was foretold: that in the last times ills are multiplied, misfortunes are diversified and, with the approach of the day of judgment, God's angry punishment moves towards the ruin of men. You are mistaken, in your foolish ignorance of the truth, when you protest that these things happen because we do not worship the gods; they happen because you do not worship God.'

Two themes are mingled in Cyprian. On the one hand is the analysis of the Roman crisis, a pessimistic picture with rhetorical, especially Sallustian, colouring and with biological motifs: old age, as in Seneca the Elder and in Florus, and certain climatological and geographical observations which might remind one of modern thinkers like the geographer Ellsworth Huntington and the chemist Liebig. On the other hand there is the idea of the imminent end of the world with the coming of Antichrist. They are the two expressions of human anguish in this tormented period of the Roman Empire: pessimistic observation and apocalyptic certainty. The first applies to categories which are more or less linked with the framework of ancient tradition. The second, which transforms the end of the state into the end of Time, is infused by the Christian sense of tragedy and stretches towards the future, burning the past behind it.

3

'External Enemies' and 'Internal Enemies'

Another Christian writer of the third century, Commodian, was the first to introduce the Germans, or more precisely the Goths, into the literature of the world as protagonists in the fall of Rome. In the reign of Decius, a stern persecutor of the Christians, the Goths had invaded and plundered the Balkan peninsula, and the Emperor himself died in 251 in a fierce battle among the marshes at Abrittus. In 252–3 the flood of the Gothic invasion touched Asia Minor and extended as far as Ephesus. It was under the impression of these events and of those which followed, including the new persecution of the Christians unleashed by Valerian in 257–8 and that emperor's ill-fated Persian War, that Commodian, about 260 approximately, wrote his *Carmen Apologeticum*. He could not bring himself to believe that a great part of the Roman world had remained deaf for two centuries and more to the message of the Christian faith; in another work he asked scornfully, 'Why have you been children (only children can believe in the thunderbolts of Jove) for two hundred years?'[1] In the *Carmen Apologeticum* his scorn for the persecuting emperor overflowed. The splendid lines of poetry were invaded from time to time, briefly and tumultuously, by a burning desire for revenge and a longing to see justice done. He wrote with

[1] This passage is crucial for the important and difficult question of the chronology of Commodian. For this see, for example, Courcelle, *Histoire Littéraire des Grandes Invasions Germaniques* (1948), pp. 127 ff. (with different conclusions from ours).

disdain of the pagans who had been taken prisoner by the barbarians and with implied delight of the invading Goths who had made friends with Christians. To the King of the Goths, Kniva, he gave the name Apollyon, 'the destroyer', taken from the Book of Revelations. The barbarian invasion became part of the apocalyptic picture of the end of the empire, expected to take place in the near future.

Commodian was not, of course, the first writer to introduce the Germans into classical literature. As early as the time of Alexander the Great, a traveller from Marseilles, Pytheas, had spoken of these Northern peoples; and about 200 B.C. a Greek collection of 'strange things'[1] had made obscure references to the *Germara*, peoples of the extreme North, 'who never see the light of day', ethnically akin to the Celts. Eratosthenes and Poseidonius had given information about the Germanic world. Caesar[2] distinguished these peoples from the Celts, emphasizing amongst other things the absence of a priestly class among the Germans, a feature which indeed is of very great importance for the history of their culture. In A.D. 98 Tacitus[3] had drawn his picture of the germanic 'virtues', connecting them with the 'ancestral way of life' of the Romans which he considered to have been obscured by the more recently developed 'legalism' and other effects of civilization. But even Tacitus's valuation of germanic characteristics was not altogether original; it was connected in various ways with Poseidonius's distinction between nature and culture, between the savages and decadent cultivation, and this was a Stoic doctrine, expressed not only in Poseidonius but also in the famous ninetieth letter of the philosopher Seneca. We should not therefore press too far the Tacitean distinction between germanic 'virtues' on the one hand and the legalistic decadence of the Romans on the other; Tacitus would have expressed approval of the 'virtues' of any other people in a state of nature, for instance of the indomitable Britons, whose *ferocia* he emphasized in contrast with the 'softness' engendered by long peacefulness.

[1] Known from an edition, which has not survived, of the *de mirab. ausc.* of the Pseudo-Aristotle (four other versions of this have come down to us), used by Stephanus Byzantinus, s.v. Γέρμαρα (or from its source).

[2] Walser, *Historia*, Einzelschr., Heft 2.

[3] Walser, *Rom, das Reich und die fremden Völker in der Geschichtschreibung der frühen Kaiserzeit* (1951).

Only the view of the Christians, directed towards the future like that of all creative minorities, could perceive (more than a century and a half after Tacitus) the position of the Germans as the leading people of modern history, set over against Rome. And that insight came, one must remember, to a poet of the highest genius[1] (for such Commodian was), who saw the judgment of God in the blasphemous grimaces of the persecuting Romans. So the revolutionary spirit of this intransigent Christian met with the new peoples who were to make history in the centuries now beginning, and indeed were already making history as they fell in fury upon the cities of the old empire. In some ways the new faith could be more easily received by these peoples than by the old classical states, which had been shaken to the core by the great spiritual upheaval of Christianity but were still bound by the external and official forms of a powerful tradition. The conversion of the Visigoths to Christianity was in fact initiated by those Christian families which had 'fraternized' with them in the third century, during the invasion. In his imagination Commodian transformed the invasion of the Goths into a menace directed against 'Rome', against the whole empire; an eager, feverish wishfulness made him leap ahead of events. In reality, a century and a half later, Alaric's Goths (Christians by this time, no longer pagans like those described by Commodian) would strike suddenly at an empire which was no longer persecuting the Christians.

'The beginning of the end will be our seventh persecution: behold it is already knocking at the door and presses on with the sword: [as a divine punishment] it will carry across the river the Goths breaking in [to the empire]. With them will be the king Apollyon, terrible in name, who in the midst of the fighting will end the persecution of the Christians. He moves towards Rome with many thousands of men and by God's decree he subdues them and takes them prisoner. Many of the senators, made prisoner, will weep then; conquered by the barbarian they blaspheme the God of heaven.

'These pagan [Goths] however everywhere nourish the Christ-

[1] One recalls the judgment of Huysmans: 'un seul poète chrétien, Commodien de Gaza, représentait dans sa bibliothèque l'art de l'an III. . . . Ces vers tendus, sombres, sentant le fauve . . .'.

ians, whom they seek out gladly as brothers, preferring them to the luxurious worshippers of false idols. In fact the Goths persecute the pagans and place the senate under their yoke. These evils descend upon those who have persecuted the Christians. Within five months the persecutors are slain by the enemy.'

In his understanding of the rôle of the Germans in the history of the empire, Commodian remains an isolated figure in the third century. About the same time another great Christian writer, Dionysius Bishop of Alexandria, contented himself with a definition of the decadence of the empire in terms of demographic crisis on the one hand and of an apocalyptic extinction of the human race on the other.

'They marvel and wonder whence come the continual plagues, the deaths of all kinds, whence comes the varied and enormous depopulation. They ask why the city now contains altogether–including the children and the aged–a population barely equal to that of the old people alone in past time. The fact is that the number of men between forty and seventy then surpassed the number of men today between fourteen and eighty. Today the youngest are the companions of the eldest.'

Behind all Christian pessimism, violent like Commodian's or reflective like that of Dionysius, there was however the eschatological conviction of the end of the world, more or less near but in any case certain. This ending seemed to be guaranteed by scripture –the Book of Daniel and the Book of Revelations. Therefore the pagans tried to attack these books which seemed almost to unite in themselves the whole suppressed protest of the followers of Christ. About 269 Porphyry, who knew the sacred writings of Christianity well, directed his attack against the fundamentals in his famous polemic *Against the Christians*, his swansong. In the twelfth book of this work he tried to show that the Book of Daniel could give no certainty about the decadence and imminent end of the empire of Rome. With the astonishing penetration which made him the greatest orientalist of antiquity he perceived that in this text the last of the 'four monarchies' points to the Seleucid and not at all to the Roman empire. The Book of Daniel, he concluded, did not contain a prophecy of the collapse of the Roman world, it simply expressed the tensions between Judaism and Hellenism in the second century

B.C. But philological researches cannot prevail over great spiritual revolutions. The ecclesiastical tradition of that age continued to seek in the Book of Daniel confirmation of the unalterable condemnation of the empire of Rome. Christian authors like Eusebius, Apollinarius and Methodius of Olympus also wrote with this conviction. About 407 St. Jerome summed up this point of view in his famous *Commentary on Daniel*:

'We assert what all ecclesiastical writers have handed down to us: at the end of the world, at that time when the kingdom of the Romans must be destroyed, there will be ten kings who will divide the Roman world. . . .'

When St. Jerome was writing the *Commentary on Daniel* the emperors had been Christian for nearly a century. Constantine, who was master of Rome from October 312, had been converted to the Christian God, abandoning the pagan devotion which was still perpetuated in the juridical structure. The old traditionalist circles, which even before the time of Constantine blamed the Christians for the Roman crisis, continued in their isolated position to speak of decadence. They did not protest openly about the christianization of the state which had taken place, but, reviving the old astrological calculations, they predicted that Christianity would have a life corresponding to a 'great year' of 365 years.[1] Above all they protested against Constantine who had introduced a new bureaucracy and police. It was to the latter that the historian Aurelius Victor attributed the 'ruin' of the Roman state.[2] And so the idea of Roman decadence, which for the Christians was now a question of biblical exegesis, came to be for the pagans the obsession of a sick man who wants at all costs to be cured. For Julian the Apostate the empire was 'sick', as he said, and in decline. He strove to give the rusty tradition a new content. One of the inhabitants of Julian's world of ideas was a critic of Constantine (and therefore probably a pagan) who addressed to an unknown emperor (apparently Constantius II) a work in which he advanced proposals for economic reforms, for reforms of the bureaucratic structure, and for new military devices. We do not know this writer's name, but

[1] Hubaux, *Antiquité Classique* (1948), pp. 143 ff.

[2] Hence the antithesis Diocletian-Constantine; cf. the present writer's *Aspetti Sociali del quarto secolo* (1951); Seston, *Reallexikon für Antike und Christentum* (1955), pp. 1036–7.

he has undoubtedly given us interesting evidence of the way in which the idea of 'decadence' was adapted by those who were most concerned about the preservation of the Roman state. Their extremely intelligent recognition of the actual facts did not change their surprising capacity for self-sacrifice. The anonymous author of this work took the new economic and social conditions as his starting point in order to deduce his proposals from them.

'It was in the age of Constantine that extravagant grants assigned gold instead of bronze (which earlier was considered of great value) to petty commercial transactions; but the greed I speak of is thought to have arisen from the following causes. When the gold and silver and the huge quantity of precious stones which had been stored away in the temples long ago reached the public, they enkindled all men's possessive and spendthrift instincts. And while the expenditure of bronze itself–which, as I have said, had been stamped with the heads of kings–had seemed already vast and burdensome enough, yet from some kind of blind folly there ensued an even more extravagant passion for spending gold, which is considered more precious. This store of gold meant that the houses of the powerful were crammed full and their splendour enhanced to the destruction of the poor, the poorer classes of course being held down by force. But the poor were driven by their afflictions into various criminal enterprises, and losing sight of all respect for law, all feelings of loyalty, they entrusted their revenge to crime. For they often inflicted the most severe injuries on the Empire, laying waste the fields, breaking the peace with outbursts of brigandage, stirring up animosities; and passing from one crime to another supported usurpers whom they brought forth for the glorification of Your Virtuous Majesty: it was not bravado that inspired them.

'Therefore, Most Excellent Emperor, you will take care in your prudence to limit public grants and thereby look to the taxpayers' interests and transmit to posterity the glory of your name. Wherefore, do you reflect for a little on the story of those happy times, and ponder upon those famous kingdoms of antique poverty, which had learned to till the fields and abstain from riches: remember how their uncorrupted frugality commends them to all history with honour and praise. Assuredly we term "golden" those realms which had no gold at all.

'Among the intolerable mischiefs from which the state suffers is the debasement of the solidus arising from the fraudulent practices of certain persons. . . . For the unscrupulous cunning of the purchaser of the solidus and the pernicious dilemma of the seller have combined to introduce considerable difficulty into the actual contracts so as to preclude the possibility of straight dealing in business transactions. Therefore your Majesties' correction must be applied in this matter, too, as in all others: I mean, the workers of the Mint must be assembled from every quarter and concentrated in a single island so as to improve the utility of the coinage and the circulation of the solidi. Let them, in fact, be cut off for all time from association with the neighbouring land, so that freedom of intercourse, which lends itself to fraudulent practices, may not marr the integrity of a public service. Confidence in the Mint will there be maintained unimpaired thanks to its isolation; there will be no room for fraud when there is no opportunity for trade. . . .

'Now in addition to these injuries, wherewith the arts of avarice afflict the provinces, comes the appalling greed of the provincial Governors, which is ruinous to the taxpayers' interests. For these men, despising the respectable character of their office, think that they have been sent into the provinces as merchants, and are all the more burdensome in that injustice proceeds from the very persons from whom a remedy should have been expected. And as if their own iniquity were not enough, everyone of them directs in the work of ruin Exactors of such character that they completely exhaust the resources of the taxpayers by various methods of extortion–evidently the Governors assume that they would be insufficiently distinguished were they alone to transgress. . . .

'I have now described, as I intended, the distresses of the State, which should rightly be removed by Imperial measures. Let us now turn to the vast expenditure on the army which must be checked similarly, for this is what has thrown the entire system of tax payment into difficulties. But in case one as busy as Your Majesty should be wearied by such a mass of confusion, I shall explain the solution of this chronic problem briefly. [Instead of twenty or twenty-five years as usual] A member of the forces, after completing some years' service and attaining to a rate of five annonae or more, should be granted an honourable discharge and go into retirement to enjoy his leisure, so that he may not burden the State by receiving these annonae any longer. . . . This procedure will not only relieve the state, oppressed as it is by its expenditure, but will also diminish the worries of the Imperial Foresight. Further, it will encourage more men to enter the service, men who were formerly deterred by the slowness of promotion.'[1]

Behind these proposals and admonitions, followed by projects for new types of military machines, there is of course one preoccupation which is especially underlined: the author wants the empire to exploit to the maximum extent its resources of manpower. These had been seriously diminished in the countryside, and therefore in the army, which was recruited from the peasantry; and at the same time, beyond the *limes*, as the anonymous author said, the barbarians 'were barking about'. If, as we suppose, the author was writing under Constantius II, a little before the coming of Julian in 361, one might say that in this respect he was relatively fortunate; he did not see, or at least he had not yet seen, the decisive onslaught of the barbarians on their immense prey. But the thought that the great calamity might overtake the empire one day made him reflect on it again and again.

It is easy for us today to smile at proposals like the enforced isolation of the moneyers. Our age is too disabused to believe that the sick will rise from their beds after a sudden cure. But these men—the anonymous author who wrote under Constantius II, Julian the Apostate, and many others too—loved their state to the point of madness. They loved it no less immoderately than Commodian and Arnobius had hated it; for the empire of Rome could in reality be the object of infinite love as well as infinite hatred. Therefore even desperate proposals like that of the island of moneyers deserve our respect. So does the despair of Julian, burning his fleet on the Tigris because of the mirage of a great pitched battle. Moreover the proposals of the anonymous writer were in some cases most intelligent: his request for deflation was carried into effect by Julian; his proposal for an army of wage-paid peasantry anticipated by two

[1] Thompson, *A Roman Reformer and Inventor* (1951); cf. Andreotti, *Rivista di Filologia Classica* (1953), p. 164. It is worth emphasizing, in so far as it affects the chronology, that *tyrannus* could only be the usurper; a man like Firmus could not be described as *tyrannus*.

centuries and a half the creation of the 'themes' by Heraclius.[1] But we should respect above all his far-seeing sadness. In 375 the catastrophe began.

As before in the time of Commodian, the movements of the peoples threatened the classic heart of the empire. In 375 there was danger of war in Italy; St. Ambrose's brother Satyrus hastened to return to Milan from Africa, where he was at the time. In another part of the empire the Emperor Valens received the Goths as mercenary troops. When coexistence with the barbarians proved to be impossible–and the fault certainly lay with the Roman ruling classes, animated by a profound hatred for the new guests–the conflict between Romans and Goths could not be avoided; in 378, after one of the most dramatic of military campaigns, Valens was defeated and died at Adrianople. To placate the victors, Theodosius, the successor of Valens, had to grant them the military command of Illyricum. Under the influence of the catastrophe men returned to questioning themselves about the deeper reasons for the disaster. A panegyrist, Themistius, was pleased to minimize these ills: in an oration dating from the beginning of 381, he showed himself content that Theodosius should have ceded the Illyrican provinces to the barbarians.

[1] The assessment of Heraclius's introduction of the themes is most important for the understanding of both Roman and medieval history; Heraclius stands just on the boundary between antiquity and the 'Byzantine Middle Ages'. This great Byzantine emperor, who ruled from 610 to 641, had to submit to the Arab advance which took Egypt and Syria from the empire, but he was able to throw back the Persian advance which threatened to submerge the whole of Asia Minor. And this success was undoubtedly due to the introduction of the themes. Heraclius set up districts in which he assigned 'property for soldiers' to the troops, with hereditary title. Each district was called a *thema*, a 'body of armed men'. There has been much debate about the origin of Heraclius's reform. The most generally held view (most recently in G. Ostrogorsky, *History of the Byzantine State*, trans. J. Hussey (1956), pp. 87 ff.) traces it back to the *limitanei* ('confinarii', soldiers on the frontiers) of the late empire. If this is correct, Heraclius's reform would not be a true innovation but would have continued Roman institutions which were already in being in the fourth century A.D. But in reality the *limitanei* of the late empire were never as a matter of rule soldier-tenants (cf. Seston, *Historia* (1955), pp. 284 ff.; Jones, *Classical Review* (1953), p. 114. Another view is put by Van Berchem, *L'armée de Diocletien et la reforme constantinienne* (1952). The chief evidence adduced by Van Berchem is, however, a passage in which the Byzantine historian Malalas says that Diocletian put the *duces* 'more within the encampments'; if, as I believe, the expression of Malalas refers solely to those 'inner boundaries' mentioned by Ammianus, XXIII, 5, 1, one may draw the conclusion that the *duces* also are at the *limes*, even if at an inner line, and that therefore the *limitanei* are not, as the distinguished Swiss historian thinks, peasant soldiers, distinct from the other soldiers proper).

The hypothesis which always faced the Christians was that the catastrophe might in truth signify not only the decadence but the coming end of the world. Commenting, in 386–8, on Jesus's prophecy of the destruction of the temple of Jerusalem and of the *consummatio saeculi*, the Bishop of Milan, St. Ambrose, drew a balance of the tragedy. On the one hand his acute sense of politics saw clearly the seriousness of the *insurrectio* of the Huns against the Alans, of the Alans against the Goths, in fact of the whole migration of peoples; on the other hand he announced a moral crisis which, in his usual manner, he painted in biblical colours. He spoke therefore of external enemies and internal enemies, *hostes extranei et hostes domestici*. By a strange chance he thus concurred with Polybius, who had spoken (though on an exclusively historical plane) of eventual 'external causes' and 'internal causes' of the decadence of Rome. (A modern reader will immediately be reminded of Toynbee's categories of 'external proletariat' and 'internal proletariat', but these are sociological predicates in Toynbee, generic concepts in St. Ambrose.) The Bishop of Milan, a completely loyal Christian subject of the emperor, regarded the acceptance of barbarian ways by a bishop as plain sacrilege and recognized the Goths in the people of Magog of whom Ezekiel had spoken. They were the *hostes extranei* (external enemies) while the *hostes domestici* (internal enemies) were the passions–above all the longing for money and authority–which had diverted men from their primitive path and ultimately from the law of nature.[1]

'The best proofs of these celestial words are ourselves, who bear the stamp of the end of the world. How many wars and what reports of catastrophe will be ascribed to us! The Huns turn against the Alans, the Alans against the Goths, the Goths against the Taifali and Sarmati. Exiled from their homes, the Goths have made us in Illyricum exiles in our own homeland. And the end of all this is not yet in sight. There is famine on all sides and plague attacks men and oxen and other beasts equally, so that even we who were not directly injured by the war find ourselves reduced by pestilence to the same condition as those who were defeated. We are indeed in the twilight of this world and therefore some of the

[1] For the understanding of the whole of 'Christian historical apologetics', one may consult the fundamental essay by Straub, *Historia* (1950), pp. 52 ff.

world's evils come first: famine is an evil of the world, pestilence is an evil of the world, persecution is an evil of the world.

'But there are also other wars which the Christian must face: the battles of rival greeds, and the conflicts of passions. The enemies within are much more serious than those without. . . . But the strong man says: though an host should encamp against me, my heart shall not fear: though war should rise against me, in this will I be confident [Psalm 26].'

In the years when St. Ambrose was writing these lines, Ammianus Marcellinus was working on his *Annals*, the most famous and most profound historical work to be produced in the late empire. He was a pagan from Antioch, but he did not write with the purpose of supporting his own beliefs. He believed in the possibility of 'objective' historical writing. Like St. Ambrose he had no love for the Germans; for example, the primitive initiation ceremonies of the Taifali appeared to him as thoroughly immoral. He tried to explain the origins of the onrush of barbarian peoples, which had thrown everything in its path into confusion, by means of an analysis of the way of life of the Huns; and he was sufficiently objective to recognize that the disaster of Adrianople had been in a certain sense willed by the Roman ruling class which had given dog meat to the Goths in return for their sons who had been reduced to slavery. He saw the origin of Roman decadence in an excessive growth of bureaucracy and oppressiveness of taxation. Therefore his disapproval fell upon Constantius II and his admiration–restrained, however, within definite limits–was reserved for Julian who, as Caesar in Gaul, had reduced the tribute from 25 solidi to 7. His attitude was on the same plane as that of the anonymous writer, mentioned earlier, who had upbraided Constantine for the excessive issue of gold and the governors for their 'appalling greed . . . ruinous to the taxpayers' interests'. Fundamentally Ammianus's work was an epic of the *res publica* which was in danger of having the life squeezed out of it by the barbarian hordes pressing on the frontiers and enrolled in the imperial army, by the desertions and treacheries of the soldiers, by the miseries which humiliated the urban life of Rome, and by the struggles for the Roman episcopal throne. Every episode and page of his *Annals* seems to lead back ideally to the thought of the catastrophe of Adrianople (378). Ammianus was writing in the age of the Emperor Theodosius the Great (379–95) which was dominated by the memory of that battle with the horrifying final scene of the defeated emperor burnt in the fire. And another who seems to have lived in the time of Theodosius[1] was Vegetius, a much lesser writer than Ammianus but nevertheless obsessed like him by the idea of the grievous decadence of Rome.

Ammianus was a pagan; Vegetius, formally at least, a Christian. But both wrote as if in the midst of an oppressive emptiness and with the obscure sense that something had been lost after 375: Ammianus with the implacable melancholy of the great historian, Vegetius with the learned optimism of one who throws out impossible solutions and plays with magic names which have by now become mere shadows of what they had been. The venerated word which came to represent for him a panacea was the 'legion'. For him the remedy for decadence was the old legionary discipline; a remedy whose vagueness and abstractness does indeed contrast with the proposals of the anonymous author who wrote under Constantius II, proposals which had been sometimes utopian but still alive and up to date. As for explanation of the crisis, Vegetius justly looked for it in the indifference of landed proprietors who avoided sending their better tenants to the levies and instead offered unfit people who would not be suitable for field work either. This was in the last analysis a precise diagnosis of the trouble–but an antiquarian remedy. Though, however, his diagnosis of the decadence has been forgotten, some of his military precepts are still familiar to our ears and, while they have remained Vegetius's own up to a point, they were in part adopted by Machiavelli.

These outworn proposals of Vegetius were then not so much remedies as contributions to the literary lamentations about decadence. As such they were also a comfort to those who wished to forget that Theodosius the Great had had to quarter the Gothic soldiers, the victors of Adrianople, in the Illyrican region in the very heart of the empire. Vegetius's scholarly labours allowed his readers to conclude that the crisis of Rome was not a new thing, since even the age of Hannibal–or so this author assured them–had seen something similar 'in consequence of the long peace which followed

[1] For the chronology of Vegetius cf. the indications in Giannelli-Mazzarino, *Trattato di Storia romana*, II (1956), pp. 542–3.

the First Punic War'. But when the Moor Gildo rebelled against Rome the danger began to be deeply felt, so that even Claudian, poet of the general Stilicho, confessed that 'the very bastion of Rome harms the empire'. Gildo was overcome. In 401 and 402 Stilicho defeated Alaric in Italy. Nevertheless the Romans of this age had to make something of an effort to believe the panegyrical effusions of the paganizing Claudian rather than the pessimism of the Christian Sulpicius Severus, who about 400 brought to mind that the feet of the statue of Nebuchadnezzar were of clay. In 406 Stilicho defeated the Ostrogoth Radagaisus but in the same year waves of barbarians poured over Gaul and some of them later into Spain: Alans, Suevi and Vandals. A section of the empire began to fall apart.

And then in 408 Stilicho was killed; in 410 Alaric took Rome. On Alaric's death his Visigoths went back up Italy into Gaul. Orientius, a man of the world who had turned religious under the weight of the tragedy, wrote his *Commonitorium* about this time: 'All Gaul', he said, 'has become one funeral pyre.'

It was not just the decadence but the collapse of the empire. Orientius's *Commonitorium* took the origin of the evil to be simply the first grievous sins: lust, envy, avarice, anger, lying. At the end of the *Commonitorium* come the four final experiences: death, hell, heaven, the last judgment. One might say that with this little poem, stretching out to the life beyond, the Middle Ages begin–nine centuries later the same motif of sin and the four last things will supply the medieval spiritual synthesis which is also the greatest poetical work of Christianity, the Divine Comedy. With Orientius the idea of decadence passes beyond the sphere of proposals and forecasts to become a terrified remorse in the presence of sin, a pure expectation of divine judgment.

'Why go over the funeral ceremonies of a world falling into ruins in accordance with the common law of all that passes away? [Here again then the echo of Sallust's *omnia orta intereunt.*] Why dwell on the number of those who die in the world, when you yourself see your own last day drawing near? . . . Blessed is he who, considering this solemn judgment, watched for by the city and the nations, can await it with a steady heart and a calm view, secure in the innocence of his life.'

In 416 another Christian poet of Gaul wrote the celebrated

Carmen de providentia, in which the idea of the 'judgment of God' and the 'heavenly city' sets the tone for a general review of recent disasters and the condemnation of sinners.

'This man weeps over the gold and silver which he has lost; this other over the furniture which was snatched from him, for the necklaces which the brides of the Goths have divided amongst themselves. . . . But you who weep over your lands, over your abandoned houses, over the avenues of your burnt castle, would you not do better to weep over your real evil, if you could see the devastation which is at your heart's core? . . .

'Let us not raise up against us, with furious lamentation, the just anger of God; let us not accuse the judgment of God, which surpasses the means of our reason and our rage more than does the bottomless abyss.'

4

The Judgments of God as an Historical Category[1]

St. Ambrose had spoken of 'external enemies', the barbarians, and of 'internal enemies', sins. The *Commonitorium* of Orientius and the *Carmen de providentia* gave first place to the internal enemies.

The idea of decadence, now strengthened by a profound sense of guilt, was transformed into the idea of the judgments of God. The historical work of Orosius, finished about 418, is woven out of 'judgments of God'. Orosius was a Spanish priest, very devoted to St. Augustine, who had known at first hand in his own country the devastations and horrors of the barbarian migrations. 'I saw the barbarians', he said, 'and I had to avoid them because they were harmful, to flatter them because they were the masters, to pray to them though they were infidels, to flee them because they laid traps.' But even this tragedy of his own life and of Roman life in the overrun provinces seemed to him nothing in comparison with the great flux of history.

'[Alexander and the Macedonians] first afflicted [the Persians] with wars and then regulated them with new laws. [The barbarians] too are now troubling with acts of war regions in which, if they were

[1] For the whole of this chapter cf. Spörl, *Grundformen Hochmittelalterlicher Geschichtsanschauung* (1935); Kamlah, *Christentum und Geschichtlichkeit* (second ed., 1951).

to succeed in maintaining themselves there–which God forbid!–they would be compelled to establish an order of their own kind so that those who are now regarded as the cruellest enemies would come to be called kings in the future. Whatever name one may wish to give to these expeditions, whether they are regarded as our ills or as the military virtue of the barbarians, in any case they remain inferior to comparable events of ancient times and in both cases they may suitably be compared with the struggle between Alexander and the Persians. If we consider them as military virtue our enemies are inferior in that respect to Alexander: if we consider them in the light of resulting evils, those endured by the Romans are less severe than those of the Persians when they were conquered by Alexander.'

This work, called for by St. Augustine and based on the idea of the four monarchies of the Book of Daniel, may be considered as an interpretation in terms of universal history of the chronological elements, deduced from the synchronism of sacred and profane history, which Christian thought had already elaborated in the age of Severus Alexander. Sacred and profane history are distinguished. From the point of view of the 'judgments of God' which are revealed in both, however, they are inseparable. In this interpretation there is a judgment of God corresponding to each Roman fault. For example, the persecution of Valerian leads to the barbarian devastation:

'of which small and poor places in various provinces still conserve the saddest traces and reminiscences in names amongst the ruins of great cities. We will point out some indeed in our own Spain as a comfort from the recent evils.'

This brings out how the classical idea of *consolatio* meets the new and completely Christian idea of the judgments of God. For Orosius the recent barbarian migrations seem to be the most evident of God's judgments and it may be said of them that 'they have occurred as penalty for the Roman guilt' (*poenaliter accidisse*), in fact as a penalty for the persecution of Diocletian. The whole Orosian interpretation of imperial history moves on this plane. For him Constantine is the emperor through whose work God sends his pagans the 'tenth plague':

'This king felt and tested the power of God and *feared* and therefore permitted the people of God to go free; this king felt and tested the power of God and *believed* and therefore permitted the people of God to go free.'

The rhythmic rules of high rhetoric have given these words a grave and moving solemnity. In other places too parallelism and *homoeoteleuton*, traditional stylistic forms, but now converted into a hieratic expressiveness, give a magical power to the judgments of God which Orosius evokes in an atmosphere of gloom and suffering, and almost pathological fervour. Divine mercy swooped against the impious Julian; Valens was burnt alive at Adrianople 'by the just judgment of God'; in the battle of Frigidus against Eugenius and Arbogast, Theodosius won the most splendid victory to be found in Roman history since the foundation of the city; Radagaisus, a pagan Goth, was defeated by divine intervention while Alaric, a Goth but a Christian, succeeded in conquering pagan Rome. Orosius has no hesitation in condemning Stilicho and his poet Claudian; Stilicho, whose son meditated the persecution of the Christians, is a traitor by nature, and Claudian is *paganus pervicacissimus*.[1]

Orosius shows more understanding for the barbarian invaders. As we saw, he does not exclude the possibility that one day their chiefs may appear as 'great kings', founders, we should say, of Romano-Germanic states. He tries to reduce the gravity of Alaric's sack of Rome. He compares the two years of barbarian outrage in Spain with the two hundred years of violence which the Spaniards had once endured at the hands of the Romans. But above all, 'there are Romans' he says 'who prefer to live in poverty-stricken freedom among the barbarians rather than to support the weight of the tribute among the Romans'. He thought that he could see something splendid, indeed unique in the whole of world history, in the peace which the Gothic king Vallia wished to make with the Emperor Honorius. A famous passage of Orosius in which he quotes the authority of St. Jerome, with whom he had close relations, attributes a remarkable conception to Ataulf, the predecessor of Vallia. Since the Goths, because of their barbarism, cannot obey laws and yet a state without laws is no true state, it is impossible to substitute a Gothia for a Romania. Therefore Ataulf seeks no more than to be the restorer of the Roman name rather than the creator of a new order.[2] About

[1] Schmid, *Reallexikon für Antike und Christentum*, III, pp. 113 ff.

[2] An original interpretation of this passage in Orosius has recently been given by

Vallia himself, Orosius can say something less ideological and more precise.

'He offered his own hazard for the sake of Roman security, offering to fight with his own forces against the other barbarians settled in Spain and to conquer them for the Romans. Besides this the other kings of the Alans, Vandals and Suevi made the same agreement with us, saying to the Emperor Honorius: *You make peace with us all and accept hostages from all of us* [*barbarians*] *and we will fight each other, we will kill each other, but we will conquer in your name, a great benefit to your state if all of us disappear in this way.* Who would believe these things if the facts did not confirm them?'

Orosius's optimism may surprise the modern reader, it may perhaps even appear grotesque, but in this case his optimism grasped one of the many truths about this absurd and contradictory epoch in which a barbarian can be a sworn enemy of a barbarian and both can be allies and destroyers of the greatest empire of the world. The empire is universal but the barbarian world is divided by conflicts full of significance for the future. With his powerful mind, inspired by the Augustinian vision of the city of God, Orosius has penetrated into the centuries to come, created a historical yardstick which will go through the whole medieval period. Starting from a polemic against the pagans who cannot renounce the old world, this priest, who has been persecuted by the barbarians, ends by exalting peace between the barbarians and his own emperor. The Augustinian conception of the world, in the final analysis, culminates in the total acceptance of history as the history of the judgments of God. 'And since' Orosius says, 'the judgments of God are ineffable and we cannot know them all or explain those which are known to us, I shall say briefly that the punishment of God the judge, in whatever form it occurs, falls justly on those who do not know.' With this presupposition the idea of decadence is in fact minimised, reduced to the pure guilt of those on whom divine judgment has swooped. Stripped of its mythical content and of its relation to contemporary events, the thought of Orosius leads to the conclusion that history is all divine, that each event speaks directly

Straub, *Unser Geschichtsbild* (1954), pp. 65–6. Cf. in general the monograph of Lippold, *Rom und die Barbaren in der Beurteilung des Orosius* (typescript dissertation, Erlangen, 1952); *idem*, *Rheinisches Museum* (1954,) pp. 254 ff.

to God. By channels which are sometimes extremely complex and contradictory, sometimes clear, his thought leads to Hegel and Ranke. His exaltation of the present (the *Christiana tempora*) as against the past, is basically a first acceptance of the actual as the divinely rational. Classical thought, which exalted the past and trembled at the idea of decadence could not have understood Orosius of course, but equally it could not have understood Hegel or Ranke.

Classical thought was still alive in the West in the minds of some pagan members of the aristocracy. For some of them it had been reduced to a traditionalism loaded with imaginary ideas or formulas. Thus, in revising the lives of the emperors in the so-called *Historia Augusta*, one of these, who seems to have lived in the age of Honorius, had emphasized the great misfortune of the 'boy-emperors' (as if Valens or Theodosius, the victim and the friend of the Goths, had been boys), and in introducing the half tragic and half crude figure of Maximinus Thrax had been happy to invent a Gothic-Alan origin for this 'tyrant' emperor. But other pagans of the West saw more vividly the drama in which they were living. They were not resigned to the abandonment of the marvellous idea of the supranational state, of the world transformed into one city and one single fatherland for all peoples. For them this beautiful fatherland must not and could not die. They blamed Stilicho for the misfortunes which had beset it, agreeing in this with the Christians, but of course for the opposite reasons. Stilicho had been a free spirit, the author of laws very favourable to Christianity but the protector of Claudian.

Of those unwilling to lose their fatherland the most outstanding was Rutilius, a spokesman of the Gallic aristocracy who turned back to Rome confident of a Renaissance. It was precisely this word, of such great importance for the history of modern European civilization, which he used: 'way of rebirth' (*ordo renascendi*). He also spoke of 'drawing a benefit from evils'. Thus, while St. Augustine was attacking Virgil's *imperium sine fine* and denying the value of the pagan *auspicium* of the eternity of Rome and Orosius was striving to interpret the work of the future 'great kings' of the barbarians, Rutilius's dream re-evoked an Augustan and Plinian phantom of eternal Rome. These fossil ideas, grandiose but already buried, were accompanied by a clearly polemical *arrière-pensée*. While the Christians were exhorting the Roman aristocracy to be converted, Rutilius was writing his famous tirade against the monks. The Roman mob, still intoxicated by the circus, kept up its pompous acclamation *Invicta Roma felix senatus.*[1]

Classical thought lived on still more in the Eastern than in the Western part of the empire. Here, under the Emperor Arcadius (395–408), Christians of pagan origin like Synesius[2] and the unyielding Christians like St. John Chrysostom were equally opposed to any concession to the barbarians. In the second half of the fifth century Zosimus, a fervent pagan, wrote his *New History* under the guidance of the works of Eunapius and Olympiodorus. There could be no greater contrast than exists between this book and the *Histories* of Orosius, a contrast which reflects the enormous difference of mentality and spiritual life which still divided the two parts of the empire more effectively than any barrier.

In the *New History* of Zosimus the classic problem of Roman decadence is again dominant. The historian cannot reconcile himself to the fall of the world which seems to be declining. He does not impute the guilt to Constantine, the hateful emperor who imposes three intolerable tributes, kills his own son, and, by the formation of the army of *comitatenses*, accustoms the soldiers to civilian life. Moreover Constantine's conversion is seen by Zosimus as something delayed. He connects it not with the campaign against Maxentius in 312, in the Christian tradition of Eusebius, but with Constantine's crimes against his own family in 326, the murder of his son Crispus and his wife Fausta. He attributes its origin to 'an Egyptian who had come from Spain'–probably, as Tillemont realized, Hosius Bishop of Cordova–and he makes the 'impiousness' of Constantine begin in 326 as a result of his conversion. In this same year Constantine was in Rome and his impiety culminates in his refusal to associate himself with the annual festival in which the army was supposed to go to the Capitol. For Zosimus impiety is of course the fatal abandonment of traditional rites. Constantine, the revolutionary emperor, always appeared in this light to the traditionalists who identified the fall of the empire with the victory of Christianity. For Zosimus, the Emperors Jovian and Theodosius are also to be counted among the great bearers of guilt. His

[1] Cf. S. Mazzarino, *Enciclopedia dell'Arte Antica*, II, under *Contorniati.*

[2] Lacombrade, *Synesios Hellène et Chrétien* (1951).

judgment on Stilicho, a completely Christian ruler but one tolerant of the pagans, is contradictory. In any case what arouses one's interest in the *New History*, and almost affects one, is the boundless and simple love of the old things.

'Polybius narrated how the Romans in a short time conquered the empire. I am about to tell how in no short time they sent it to ruin by their own fault. I shall expound these things when I have come to that point in the narrative. . . . When I have reached those times in which the empire of the Romans, in a brief space barbarized, was reduced to a small part which was also decadent (διαφθαρέν), then I shall also expound the causes of the disaster and I shall also add as far as I can the oracles which foretold such events. . . .

'[Jovian, the successor of Julian made peace (in 363) with the Persians, ceding to them Nisibis and five regions beyond the Tigris.] At this point it occurs to me to turn back to a more ancient time and to wonder if the Romans ever reconciled themselves to granting something that they had conquered to others, or if indeed they tolerated that another should have what had been at one time made part of their empire. [This never happened even as a result of the gravest of disasters, that of the campaign of Valerian.] Only the death of the Emperor Julian could lead to the loss of those territories [which Jovian ceded]. Thus up to now the Roman emperors have failed to recover any of them and moreover have in a brief time lost the greater part of the subject nations, some becoming independent, others ceded to the barbarians and yet others reduced to serious depopulation. . . .

'[When Valens (in 378) went to fight the Goths] a strange spectacle presented itself to the army which was going forth and to the emperor himself. On the road they found a wretched man whose body was quite still and apparently beaten from head to foot, but his eyes were open and watched whoever came near him. They asked him who he was and from whom he had received these injuries and, since he did not reply, they decided that they had met with something quite out of the ordinary and brought him to the notice of the emperor. The latter interrogated him but the man remained dumb. It seemed as if he were not living because his head did not move and that he was not dead because his eyes were looking. . . . But those who understood these matters said that it was the presage of the future collapse (κατάστασιν) of the state and that the commonwealth would be struck and beaten to the point of death until finally it would be destroyed by the baseness of the emperors and rulers. Considering the separate events one sees that this was truly said. . . .

'[In 380] Theodosius sent out the collectors of the public taxes to round up the tribute with the greatest thoroughness. He was acting as though the victories of the barbarians had not brought any ills at all to the cities of Macedonia and Thessaly! So one could see that if the humaneness of the barbarians had left something the tax collector would carry that off too. In fact the taxpayers had to make their payments not only in money but also with women's jewellery and with garments of all kinds, even underclothes, and as a result of this exaction of taxes city and countryside were full of laments and complaint and all invoked the barbarians and sought the help of the barbarians. . . .

'[From the year 395] by the will of Theodosius the performance of sacrifices was ended at Rome and other things were neglected which derived from ancestral tradition. For this reason the empire of the Romans decayed ["was diminished"] in part and became open to the barbarians so that finally, escaping from the control of its own inhabitants, it took on such a form that even the places where there were formerly cities are no longer recognizable.'

Zosimus's melancholy derived from this obstinate defence of the old forgotten things but he did not attain to the serenity of reflection and he is not a really great historian. Another historian who also wrote in the second half of the fifth century was Priscus, a Thracian who had taken part in the Byzantine embassy to the King of the Huns, Attila, in 449. This journey had enlarged the horizons of his conception of the great theatre of the barbarian world. He too felt the sadness of the decay but he did not consider it merely as a misfortune imposed by destiny. The barbarian invaders had been introduced into the literature of the classical peoples by a Christian poet of the third century, the Commodian of the *Carmen apologeticum*. Soon after, still in the third century, the age of the Emperor Claudius the Goth had produced a historical work by Dexippus about the Goth–'Scythians', burning with the eagerness for imperial restoration which animated the work of the Illyrian emperors.

Two hundred years after Dexippus the picture of the barbarian peoples appeared to Priscus in all the richness of its varied colours. He could not stop, as Dexippus had done, at a simple antithesis between the 'reason' (*logos*) represented by Rome and the violence (*amathia*) proper to the barbarians. It was not his task to describe restorations or Roman victories. He could still see before him the restless little eyes of Attila, lord of the Huns, terrible and yet human. And another character in his story was certainly the Vandal Genseric, the conqueror of Rome, stooping and lame, incapable of long speeches and closed in upon himself. But, above all, the power of these two and of the other barbarian kings appeared to him to be connected with the organic difficulty of avoiding the discontent amongst the inhabitants of the Roman empire. One episode brought him very close to this aspect of the crisis. On his journey to the Hun court he had gone through the old lands of Dacia, once a Roman dominion, now lost for almost two centuries and returned to barbarism. With the exception of those who had frequent contacts with the Romans on this side of the Danube, no one spoke Latin in Dacia any longer; no one spoke Greek except prisoners of Thracian or Illyrican origin. But there was one Roman whom he met and who spoke Greek to him, a refugee who had abandoned his own country and was happy to remain in the land of the Huns. Why had he fled? With sophistic relish, but also with thoughtful sadness, Priscus relates his conversation with the man who had chosen to exile himself from the world of the vine and wheaten bread. The man says: 'Among the Romans the laws do not apply to everyone. If they are broken by one of the rich he does not pay the penalty; if by a poor man he will be punished if he does not die before judgment is given against him, through the delays and expenses of the case.' Priscus replies: 'No, the laws apply to everyone, so much so that even the emperor is bound to obey them. As for the costs of cases, they are necessary to pay the expenses of the court.' There is an endless sadness in this exchange. Men prefer a happy savagery to the weight of a superior civilization. Grotius, who later contrasted the good barbarian laws with the complex laws of the Romans, would have been glad to quote this passage from Priscus.

Priscus underlines in his historical work the difference between the two parts of the empire: 'Attila was undecided which of the two empires he ought to attack. It seemed to him at last advisable to devote himself to what would be the more bitter war by marching towards the West.' Two hundred years earlier Dexippus too had observed that 'the men of the West are all more warlike than those of the other part of the empire'. But the consideration which Priscus attributes to Attila has quite a different significance. Here it is not a matter of warlike soldiers from the western Roman provinces; for Attila the western war is more bitter because it is a war against Goths. The truly Roman army is a contemptible thing in the eyes of the Hun captain and Priscus implicitly endorses this attitude. The great strength of the Roman army of the west lay in the Visigoths who were allied troops rather than auxiliaries, fighting in their own barbarian units and not allowing themselves to be romanized like the Celtic or British troops of the third century. These Visigoths defeated Attila in 451. The western part of the empire had already set out on its new road, 'barbarized' as Polybius would have said and as Zosimus was now saying.

Only the historiographical tradition initiated by Orosius, inspired by St. Augustine's *City of God*, could throw a bridge between Christianity and barbarism. Of course not all Christians loved the barbarians. The sermon *On the Barbaric Time* written in Vandal Africa and attributed to Quodvultdeus, Bishop of Carthage, who was exiled by Genseric in 439, almost foretold the disappearance of the Vandals, but at the same time it declared the new tribulations to be just.

'Yes, you tell me that the barbarian snatches everything from you. "I", you tell me, "remain in misery and he is replete with that which is not his." I see, I understand, I consider: you have been a fish placed in this sea which a greater fish has devoured. Wait a while. A still greater fish will come to devour him who devoured, to despoil him who despoiled, to take from him who has taken. In fact, although your tribulations are just–in not giving to others you have wickedly kept your own things–nevertheless you have seen and will see the sufferings of him who stole from another. This plague with which we are scourged will not last for ever. It is indeed in the hands of Omnipotent God.'

The hopes expressed in the sermon *On the Barbaric Time* were not fulfilled. The Vandals remained in Africa and made even worse attacks on the Christians so that in 488–9 Victor Bishop of Vita protested against useless sympathies with the barbarians. But in general the Orosian idea of the judgments of God had expressed adequately the Christian attitude towards the invasion. Towards the middle of that terrible fifth century Salvian of Marseilles had reaffirmed the principle that 'the Romans are enduring their punishments by the first judgment of God', and that the barbarian plundering was not as intolerable as the tributary exactions of the Romans. This was not just rhetoric; the provincials had in fact been invoking the barbarians since the time of Adrianople to liberate them from the weight of the tributes, and one recalls the Roman who declared to Priscus that he preferred the Huns to the rulers of his homeland. Men of religion, even if they were not pro-barbarian, still made themselves mediators between barbarians and Romans; like Pope Leo with Attila and St. Severinus with Odoacer and with the royal family of the Rugii. This phenomenon of religious mediation also had its prehistory from the time of Adrianople.

When Odoacer in 476 deposed the Emperor Romulus in Italy and then in 493 had to capitulate before the Ostrogoth Theodoric, these serious events put decisively in front of everyone the problem of the attitude to be adopted to the barbarians. For the idea of decadence was substituted that of collaboration between Romans and Goths for the defence of a common civilization. In this way *civilitas*, an important concept in the late empire, already used to exalt the spiritual attitude of Julian the Apostate (*civilis*, 'towards all'), entered fully into the history of Romano-Germanic Europe. 'The glory of the Goth', said Cassiodorus,[1] 'is the guardianship of *civilitas*.' Another exponent of high Roman culture, Ablavius, had already before him investigated the heroic sagas (*prisca carmina*) of the Goths, seeking points of contact between this barbarian history and the history of Rome. The invention of the *Historia Augusta* that the Emperor Maximinus had been of Gothic-Alan extraction became an accepted tradition. More recent history was falsified with more deliberate purpose. Stilicho, the bête noire of Orosius, was buried under the weight of a new charge when Cassiodorus presented him as defeated and put to flight by Alaric's Goths at

[1] On the personality of Cassiodorus see the recent work of Momigliano, *Rendiconti dell'Accademia dei Lincei* (1956), pp. 279 ff.

Pollentia. When it came to Alaric's sack of Rome in 410 Cassiodorus found a way, by applying an Orosian tradition, of emphasizing Alaric's religious side.

So little by little, in the West, the tragic memory of 410, the year of the occupation of Rome, was whittled down. To contemporaries this drama had seemed to be the sign of the end of a world, perhaps of the whole world. St. Augustine and Orosius, though contemporaries, had tried to perceive the judgments of God in it. Cassiodorus, the contemporary of Theodoric, had found in it the evidence of Alaric's Christian devotion. Jordanes, a Goth-Alan, who wrote in 551 when the Ostrogothic state had already declined, repeated the praises of Alaric which were already to be found in Cassiodorus. According to him, and perhaps according to Cassiodorus, no burning had taken place during the sack. Besides, the occupation of Rome remained a contemporary question. Totila had made two *ingressus* into Rome in 546 and 549. This was the *perditio Romae*. Gregory the Great, who was Pope from 590 to 604, was convinced that Rome could never have been destroyed by the barbarians. Looking back, we can compare these writers with each other and follow their reactions to the vicissitudes of the city which had fallen and survived. From St. Augustine to St. Gregory the Great there is a dialogue on the subject lasting for nearly two centuries. In an oration in the year 410 itself Augustine had said:

'Does it surprise you that the world is failing? You are surprised that the world grows old. Man is born, grows up, ages. There are many woes in old age. . . . If a man grows old he is full of tribulations; if the world grows old it is full of disasters. Perhaps God did not give you enough when he sent you Christ in the world's old age. . . . Do not remain bound to the old world and do not refuse to be rejuvenated in Christ who says to you "Let the world perish, let it grow old, let it fail, suffer the gasping of old age. Do not fear. Your youth shall renew itself like eagles." Yes, the pagan says, Rome is dying in the age of the Christians. Perhaps Rome is not dying: perhaps it was beaten but not killed, perhaps it was chastised but not destroyed. Perhaps Rome does not die if the Romans do not perish. They will not perish if they praise God, but they will perish if they blaspheme against Him. What indeed is Rome if not the Romans? It is not a matter of stones and planks, of high buildings and great walls. These things were made to be sometime destroyed. In building man puts stone upon stone and in destroying he takes stone from stone. A man makes these things and a man destroys them. Does one do wrong to Rome by saying that it is falling. No, not to Rome, but rather, if at all, to its creator.'

Again in the *City of God* he writes:

'What fury of foreign peoples, what barbarian cruelty, can be compared with the harm done by civil wars? . . . The Goths spared so many senators that it is rather to be marvelled that they killed a few. . . . The last list of proscriptions made by Sulla, on the other hand, not to speak of innumerable other deaths, brought death to more senators than the Goths could even have plundered [in Alaric's sack of Rome].'

In Orosius the motifs of Augustine are expanded into a coherent historical interpretation.

'After [the punishment of Stilicho and] such an increase of blasphemy and absence of repentance, there fell on the City that [divine] judgment which had been so long in suspense. Alaric comes to besiege, trouble and invade humbled Rome. However he first gives the order to leave unharmed and in peace those who had taken refuge in holy places and especially the basilicas of Peter and Paul and further that, though his men might plunder without restraint, they should abstain from the shedding of blood. . . . While the barbarians were roving about the city, by chance one of the Goths, a man of high position and of Christian faith, found in a church a virgin consecrated to God, now advanced in age, and, without offering offence, asked her for gold and silver. With Christian sureness she told him that she had a great quantity of it, sent for it to be brought to him, and showed it to him. Since the barbarian was astounded by the great weight of wealth but did not know the quality of the vessels, the virgin of Christ said to the barbarian, "These are the holy instruments of the apostle Peter. Take them if you dare. . . ." The barbarian, compelled to religious reverence by fear of God and by the virgin's faith, sent a messenger to tell these things to Alaric who ordered that all the vessels, as they were, should be carried immediately to the basilica of the Apostle and that the virgin, and with her all the Christians who should join the procession, should be conducted there under escort. . . . On the third day the barbarians left the city of their own accord after having burnt a certain number of houses, but not as many as the dwellings destroyed by mere accident in the seven-hundredth year of the foundation of the City.'

Orosius had completed his *Historiarium Libri* in 417 and his interpretation of Alaric's sack had a central position in it. When Cassiodorus was Praetorian Prefect, an office which had been entrusted to him by Amalasunta in 533, he also went over the same great events which he had already dealt with in his *Historia Gothorum.*

'When King Alaric, satisfied by the sack of the city of Rome, received from his men the vessels of the apostle Peter, and knew by inquiry what they were, he ordered that they should be returned to the sacred basilica by the same hands which had taken them, so that greed, which had caused the crime in the fury of plundering, should wipe out the mistake by showing the most complete devotion.'

Cassiodorus's account, in order to exalt still more Alaric's religious feeling, imagined that the sacred vessels had been carried before him. Jordanes, about 550, repeated Cassiodorus's interpretation.

'Finally, having entered Rome, the Visigoths limited themselves to plunder, but unlike the pagans they did not burn or allow that insults should be made in the places of the Saints.'

Gregory the Great, whose whole life centred around Rome (he was born there in 540, prefect of the city before 573, abbot of his monastery in 585, and finally pope in 590), gave a new development to the theme under the inspiration of a new and much later barbarian occupation of Rome, Totila's march through the Porta Asinaria in 546.

'[St. Benedict said to Totila:] "You will enter Rome, you will cross the sea, you will hold the kingdom for nine years, in the tenth you will die." Hearing this the king was much frightened; he withdrew asking the saint to pray for him and from that time he was less cruel. Not long afterwards he entered Rome, he went to Sicily, and in the tenth year of his reign by the judgment of God he lost, with his life, his power. Moreover the bishop of the church of Canosa used to turn to the servant of God [St. Benedict] and the man of God loved him greatly for his way of life. Speaking with the saint about the entry of Totila into Rome and about the end of the city, the bishop said, "This city will be destroyed by the work of this king so that it will no longer be inhabited". The man of God replied to him, "Rome will not be destroyed by the barbarians but will perish overthrown by thunderstorms, whirlwinds and earthquake in itself". For us the mysteries of this prophecy are clearer than day. We see in this city the walls going to ruin, the houses fallen down, the churches destroyed by the whirlwind; and the buildings crumbling from old age because ruins upon ruins tear them down.'

This ideal dialogue on the fall of Rome, begun by St. Augustine, does not stop with St. Gregory the Great.[1] Still in the age of Frederick Barbarossa, almost six and a half centuries after Gregory the Great the *Expositio* of Alexander the Minorite is dominated by the idea of *Roma capta*.

'Rome, the head of the church, was often taken, not by its own kings but by barbarians and by infidels. First indeed by Alaric of whom Augustine writes. Then again it was taken by Genseric, then by Totila, of whom Gregory writes. Then again for 14 years by Odoacer who afflicted the faithful for a long time. However the kingdom of our Lord Jesus Christ continued and grew on earth and his kingdom in eternity will have no end.'

We may now smile at the placing of Odoacer (476) after Totila (546). But in the vision of the Minorite as in all the 'historical eschatology' (if one may use this contradictory description) which dominates the medieval West, the essence of problems lies not in the reconstruction of the past but in the interpretation of the judgments of God. In this sense the whole medieval world and its literary production, which varied so much in quality, saw history with the eyes of Augustine and Orosius. Of course the Orosian motif of the four monarchies, which was illuminated also by a classicist like St. Jerome, was corrupted by the typically Augustinian motif of the six or seven ages of the world; Isidore and Bede are the other arbiters of medieval spirituality. In this perspective the end of the ancient world, identified with the end of the world, became generally speaking removed from the past and projected, so to speak, into the present or future. The foundation of the new 'Roman Empire' of the West at Christmas 800[2] only confirmed this perspective of a style which had survived beyond its own time.

[1] Cf. Manselli, *La 'Lectura super Apocalipsim' di Pietro di Giovanni Ulivi* (1955).

[2] Of the older works one should mention, in addition to the famous book by Graf, *Roma nella memoria e nelle immaginazioni del Medio Evo*, I and II (1883), the brief

The problem of the end of the ancient world became rather a problem of *translatio*. In this dimension of historical events, if at all, it was possible to feel the break caused by the Arab invasion. Medieval men tended at times to take a view akin to Pirenne's thesis; that is of course on an eschatological rather than a historical plane. Carrying the historical application of the categories of Augustine and Orosius to an extreme point one could see the history of the empire in absolute connection with ecclesiastical history, in the manner say of Hugh of Fleury. But the symbol of the epoch remained its famous invention (prior to 778), the *Constitutum Constantini*. There was endless conflict about this throughout the Middle Ages–for us the most interesting episode may be the famous criticism of Leo of Vercelli in 1001–and Constantine and Julian, on the good and bad sides respectively, dominated medieval fantasies. The *Gallicanus* of Hrosvitha was the dramatic expression of this perspective.

However the sense of decadence in this period was not limited to laments about the 'drying up' of studies or in another field to warnings against the increasing worldliness of the Church. The fascination of the vanished empire began to take the shape either of tortuous literary combinations based on Sallust or Lucan or of a sad sensibility to the empire's unique greatness in the history of the world. In the first category there are reflections like those which characterize the rhythmic composition of a canon of St. Omer, Petrus Pictor, *On the Destruction of the Roman Empire and on the Magnificence of Cato*:

'Rome, once powerful, capital of the world, glory of the countries, is now a den of thieves, its palace a poor man's shack. We would need Cato to return.'

Here all historical perspective is lost. The real concern of Petrus Pictor is his protest against simony and the corruption of the world. His Cato is a conflation of Cato the Censor with Cato of Utica and

contribution by Patetta, *Atti dell 'Accademia di Scienze di Torino* (1895). Cf. Morghen, *Medioevo Cristiano* (second ed., 1958), pp. 41 ff., 60 ff.; Dupré-Theseider, *L'idea imperiale di Roma* (1942). A new burst of studies on Carolingian symbolism has been inspired by the works of Schramm; see Deér, *Schweizer Beiträge* (1957), pp. 5 ff.; Beumann, *Historische Zeitschrift* (1958), pp. 515 ff. In particular note this point which has generally been neglected: in the prayers of Adrian I and Leo III for Charlemagne to abandon the Frankish *habitus* appear requirements expressed, about four centuries earlier, in *Codex Theodosianus*, XIV, 10, 2, 3, 4 (cf. ch. 8 below).

the author of the *Disticha Catonis*. A high degree of emotion is aroused, about the same time by the two famous poems of Hildebert of Le Mans, inspired by his journey to Rome in 1101. Here the transition from Rome, lady of the earth, to Rome, lady of heaven, is felt in the framework of a grandiose Augustinian 'rhythm'. Also Augustinian in spirit are the *imminui* of the *regnum mundi*, that is of the Roman Empire, in Otto of Freising, the uncle of Frederick Barbarossa.

One aspect of the end of the ancient world, its relation with the Arab invasions, was naturally particularly felt in the Spain of the *Reconquista*. In the thirteenth century Rodrigo of Toledo exalted the glorious tradition of the Goths, 'that conquering people, that noble people, the nation of the Goths to whom Asia and Europe had given themselves; and the African world had been ceded to the Vandals who had fled before them.' Thus Rodrigo, with a perspective which foreshadows the thesis expounded by Henri Pirenne in *Mahomet and Charlemagne*, belittles the drama of the end of Rome and accentuates that of the Arab invasion. In evoking this, Rodrigo's prose has strains of desperation which recall, as if in contrast, the lament of St. Ambrose, between eight and nine centuries earlier, for the victories of the Goths in the empire. The exaltation of the Goths by Jordanes is repeated, but by a new voice. To Rodrigo the Goths appear to be the real masters of the ancient world, the conquerors even of the Persian king Cyrus (the reference is to the queen of the Massagetae, who by a commonplace juxtaposition had also been 'transformed' into Goths) and the break introduced into the history of the world by the Arab invasion was all the sadder for this.

'Oh, Sorrow! Here ends the glory of the majesty of the Goths, in the year 752 [equivalent to A.D. 711]. That majesty which had subdued innumerable kingdoms in innumerable wars, lowered (*inclinavit*) in a single war the standards of its glory. They who with various massacres had devastated Pontus, Asia, Macedonia, Greece and Illyricum; whose queens had subjugated in wars the region of the East, and in a welter of blood had killed their defeated prisoner Cyrus, the great lord of Babylonia, Assyria, Media, Syria and Hyrcania; and Rome, lord of all the provinces, defeated, had bowed the knee to them; by whom Emperor Valens was defeated, burnt in the fire; whose empire the illustrious Attila King of the Huns recognized in the battle of the Catalaunian Plains; to whom the Alans, fleeing in battle left Pannonia and the Vandals, also in flight, abandoned the provinces of Gaul; the menacing thunders of whose wars resounded through the centuries. The rebellion of Mahomet, bursting out in a short time, overwhelmed them in one single war with unheard of slaughter.'

Beside the medieval West were the worlds of Byzantium and the Arabs. At Byzantium the interpretation of the Roman crisis was very much more closely tied to the historical events. The sense of the state was still alive and the new Rome, Constantinople, set itself the problem of the late Roman empire. The greatest of the Byzantine historians, Procopius, in a certain sense christianized the classical sense of decadence. In his *Anekdota*, written in 550, Justinian is regarded as the arch-demon. In the broad sweep of Procopius's vision,[1] in his *Wars*, there was a clear view of the events which had led to the crisis of the empire in the West and then to the restoration carried out by Belisarius. But even after Procopius the problems of the late empire remained living problems for the Byzantine historians. The polemics against Zosimus in favour of Constantine, for instance, dealt with living questions.

The Arab world is full of surprises for us. Here there is a great spiritual gap and the Roman empire is seen with eyes turned to Byzantium. In the fourteenth century a very great man, Ibn Khaldun, sums up this wonderful Arab culture, embracing a kaleidoscope of nationalities and dynasties which rise and fall. In his work there is the idea of decadence connected with city life (*hadâra*), contrasted with the life of the countryside (*badâwa*) on the other hand which calls forth *esprit de corps* (*'aṣabiyya*) and conquests. The crisis of the Roman empire of the West which culminated in the battle of Yarmuk (636) and the taking of Alexandria (646) is studied within the framework of religious values and ideals which give life to the *esprit de corps* (*'aṣabiyya*). His work is the only sociological interpretation of the end of the ancient world which was evolved during the Middle Ages and even now we can learn a

[1] On Procopins we now have the fundamental essay by Rubin (*Paulys Realencyclopädie*, XXIII, i).

lot from it. It may suggest two particular reflections. Firstly the battle of 636 was a break, which we ought to regard as the last act in the end of the ancient world which had begun with the invasions of the Goths. Secondly the decisive factor in the Roman crisis appears as the religious hostility of Nestorian Syria, and we may add monophysite Egypt, to the empire. Similarly in the West the imperial crisis is expressed in part in the fervour of the Donatist heretics in Africa. In spite of appearances Ibn Khaldun is not animated in this investigation by his pride as a Muslim. He knows perfectly well that the Muslim states, just as much as the empire of Rum, will fall 'when God wills'. With his work Polybius's 'objectivity' returns.

'The light of religion (*ṣighba dîniyya*) drives away the feelings of rivalry and envy which reign among the peoples inspired by a strong *esprit de corps* (*'aṣabiyya*). It gives all spirits a single direction in the sense of the law. If they concentrate their efforts on their own interests nothing can resist them because they all have one direction, one aim, and for this they will face death. Even if the inhabitants of the state which they are trying to capture are twice as strong the efforts of the defenders are in vain; they desert each other for fear in face of the death which comes [from attackers inspired by the light of religion]. Thus the defenders offer no resistance even if they are much more numerous and the conquerors defeat them. And decadence carries off the defenders by the comfort and corruption which reign amongst them, as we were saying. This happened in the early period of Islam when the Arabs made their conquests. At Yarmuk the Muslim army went into battle against the troops which Heraclius had collected there, whose numbers, if we believe al-Waqidi, reached 400,000 men. In those two battles nothing could hold back the Arabs. They threw the enemy into confusion and took possession of the booty.'

5

The End of Rome as interpreted by Humanism

Humanism understood at once the great upheaval that had overturned the western world in the fifth century. Petrarch in the fourteenth century was already lamenting the disappearance of those 'anime leggiadre' who had placed Rome 'là dov'ella era'; he therefore explained the fall of Rome above all by the disappearance of great men, a judgment in the spirit of Cicero.[1] 'Civic' humanism – to use the well-known phrase of the historian of Florentine political thought, Hans Baron – enlarged on this theme and the concept of the 'decline' of the Roman empire in its last period was elaborated. The 'causes' of the decline of Rome played a part in every serious humanistic dispute – Guarino said that this decline was due not to Caesar but to the corruption of manners. Rome's *inclinatio* was, in short, at the bottom of a particular way of understanding history.

In 1441 the Florentine humanist Leonardo Bruni spoke of *vacillatio*; his famous literary opponent Flavio Biondo used the word *inclinatio*, 'decline'. Biondo's chief work, completed in 1453, carried even into the title page this sense of a break between the ancient world and the 'middle age' of which Cusanus, or at least his followers, had already spoken. The book was called *Historiarum*

[1] G. Toffanin, *L'uomo antico nel pensiero del Rinascimento* (1955).

ab inclinatione Romanorum imperii decades tres, 'Histories beginning with the decline of the Empire of the Romans'. Why *inclinatio*, 'decline'? Both the concept and its name are, used in this sense, new, a sign of the extraordinary creativity of the age of humanism, which discovered not only the greatness of ancient Rome but also the sadness of its withdrawal into itself almost at the moment of its fall.

Modern scholars have made some investigations into the origins of this idea of *inclinatio* or 'decline', which has to be considered in conjunction with the later idea of 'rebirth', destined to provide such a wonderful definition of the age of Humanism and Renaissance. The general opinion today is that the concept of the 'inclinatio' of the Roman empire, from which Biondo's work starts, is modelled on the New Testament image of Jesus who expired *inclinato capite*, 'with his head bowed'. The suggestion is that in the terminology of Biondo and the humanists, Rome, as *caput mundi*, was a kind of allegorical image to which was applied the ecclesiastical formula: *tenebrae factae sunt–et inclinato capite remisit spiritum*, 'darkness came and with his head bowed Jesus gave up the ghost'. This is a fascinating and brilliant hypothesis but it does not seem quite to hit the truth. Perhaps one may suggest a simpler explanation both of the concept and of the word *inclinatio* by deriving it from the biblical idea of the power of God over the *kingdoms*, as it is formulated in Psalm 45, the song of trust in God. At verse 7 the Vulgate reads *conturbatae sunt gentes et inclinata sunt regna*. In fact in Biondo's conception the *inclinatio* of the Roman empire is above all a punishment, from that God who in the psalmist's words 'troubles the nations and bows down the kingdoms'. If this may be regarded as the primary origin of the conception, we should add to it the vivid memory, which must have been present in Biondo's mind, of the anxiety of Cicero and Sallust for the *inclinata res publica*, for a Rome which was bending under the weight of the crisis in the last period of the republic. Had not Cicero said of that Octavian who would one day become Augustus that he might have brought support to the free republic 'which almost falls and collapses', *labente et inclinatae paene res publicae*? One recalls that for Biondo another distant cause, not yet a beginning of the *inclinatio* of the Empire was just this transition from the free republic to the monarchical state of the imperial period.

If Flavio Biondo did indeed derive his idea of *inclinatio* in the way here suggested, the genesis of this conception, which was to prove itself so fruitful throughout modern historiography, would in a sense reflect the dual aspect of a part of the world of Renaissance Humanism. On one side is the attraction of the great tradition of Rome's republican liberty, expressed by Cicero in its most tragic and harrassed moment; on the other the attempt to embrace the ancient biblical wisdom, as expressed for example in the Psalms, in a serene and yet pragmatic vision of human things. Behind this complex experience there is at the same time a precious recovery of historical perspective. The sense of time, which the Middle Ages had lost in the stress towards the future, returned and dissipated the misty vision of the past in terms of an imprecise eschatology.

In the first place this now makes periodization necessary. Flavio Biondo makes the *inclinatio* of the Empire start with the sack by Alaric in 410 (which he mistakenly puts in 412). Secondly it raises the question of causes, quite distinct from that of periodization. It may be a matter of very remote causes (such as the loss of republican liberty) or just distant ones (the persecution of the Christians, the translation of the Capital to Constantinople) or finally of generic causes (the recurrence of the decline of kingdoms). Some of these 'causes', above all the emphasis on the persecution of the Christians, are derived from Orosius. But the difference between Orosius and Biondo is vital. For Orosius each persecution brings its own special revenge (Nero's persecution leads to the plague of the civil war of 69, Domitian's brings about the misery and exile of nearly all the citizens, and so on; only the tenth persecution has a distant effect up to the barbarian migrations). For Biondo the persecutions in general, and not one particular example, are all together a possible remote cause of Rome's *inclinatio*. Furthermore, the inclusion of imperial caesarism amongst the possible causes of the *inclinatio* is more in the spirit of Petrarch than in that of Orosius. The loss of republican liberty appears to Biondo as bound up with the deterioration of moral life and therefore with the coming of inferior types of humanity (*vili* and *tristi*), a very modern point of view which resembles some of the formulations of Otto Seeck (see ch. 8) and Guglielmo Ferrero (see ch. 12). The general cause itself, the changing vicissitudes of human things, has in Flavio Biondo something classical and humane about it, rather different from Orosius's rigid construction based on eschatology and numbers.

It is especially significant that Flavio Biondo can, at a distance of a millennium, narrate events for which Orosius is the principal source, and yet at the same time correct the source, or, at any rate, free it of superimposed constructions. For Biondo, as previously for Orosius, Stilicho is–nor could he be otherwise–the great protagonist of the fatal age in which the Visigothic attack was unleashed and with it the *inclinatio* of the empire. Also in Biondo, as in Orosius, Stilicho appears as a perfidious and wretched man; but in Biondo this miserable individual is portrayed as a master of military arts, so that he is no longer evil through and through. Biondo in fact brings a clearly critical approach to bear on his authors in his reconstruction of the imperial decline, not least to Orosius who is his point of departure. In the very first pages of his work, the lament for the inadequacy of the. contemporary sources of this epoch of *inclinatio*, in comparison with the classical sources for the republican period, is inseparable from his idea of the general decadence of culture in an age of eclipse and the previously mentioned inquiry into the 'causes'.

'When Rome was great its splendour was parallel with the blossoming of poets, historians and orators which accompanied its development. As soon as the crisis of the empire began with the reduction and humiliation of its power the poets, historians and orators also disappeared. Thus we have monuments of its greatness and glory which have never been equalled on earth, celebrated by the works of many and illustrious talents; but the greatest obscurity shrouds and covers its decline. . . . We say that the summit and, as it were, the apex of the empire was the age of Theodosius I and, ten years later, of his sons Arcadius and Honorius. In fact, although the Roman state had endured by that time many damages and evils, it was soon restored and returned to its ancient majestic authority. But in the tenth year of Arcadius and Honorius, after the defeat of Radagaisus at Fiesole, the dignity of the empire, which was already tending towards ruin, began to suffer a serious decadence with the very numerous inroads of the barbarians, first of all that of Alaric. . . . We shall shortly narrate these events. Now let us turn aside to refute the opinion, which many uphold, that the decadence (*in-*

clinatio) of the empire had already begun under the dictatorship of Julius Caesar. We do not accept that opinion because, on the contrary, Roman power was increased under many of the Caesars rather than reduced. In the same way I can agree that the transference (*translatio*) of the capital to Byzantium by Constantine may have been a remote cause of the decadence to come but I will never concede that it may be called the beginning of the decadence. Since I am thus bound to express an opinion on the cause and first origin of Roman decadence, I say that it is not an altogether erroneous view which sees the origin of this upheaval in the disappearance of republican liberty under Caesar; for together with liberty perished the arts of living well and piously. For the sake of the government of one man the fear of laws disappeared. The princes distrusted virtue and magnanimity and preferred the ignoble to the strong, the evil to the good, the flatterers and the corrupt to the men of character and sanctity. My judgment would not reject the opinion of those who, considering the transitoriness of the things of this world, hold that the Romans lost the empire because of that same destiny which led some other peoples and cities of almost equal greatness into serious decay: Babylonia, the Medes, Carthage, Macedonia. To speak with Orosius, we ought not to marvel if Rome, which was born servile under the kings, lost with the decemvirate the liberty previously won under the consuls and in the year 360 of its foundation was occupied and burnt by the Gauls and then, after its wonderful recovery, power and pride growing with each other and vices overcoming wealth, was torn by the civil wars (*bellis est lacerata civilibus*) and finally in its seven-hundredth year submitted to the yoke of a single ruler, Caesar. A third explanation of the fall of Rome is also proposed; I mean the religious negligence of the Romans; and I hold this to be the best explanation just because it is a religious explanation. In fact the Roman emperors in the midst of their lordly splendour raged against the Christians with most cruel torments; nor did the cruelty of the massacres or the divine omens dissuade them from this purpose. Therefore, after ten persecutions of the Christians made by edicts, they were led by the secret judgments of God to that which was the cause of the fall of the empire which they did not deserve. In fact Flavius Constantine called the Great, a most Christian prince, the instrument of divine punishment for the impiety committed by the Roman people against the Christians, was elevated by our God so that by changing the seat of the empire he weakened Rome, which was destined soon to return to that nothingness from which it had risen to power. Therefore I say that the decadence of the city, whether it is to be attributed to all the above reasons or to any one of them, had its beginning in the invasion of the city of Rome by the Goths.'

Naturally this vision of a world in decline was always suffused with an atmosphere of deep melancholy. But the humanists were always aware that the drama of the vanished ancient world could now subside into the contemplation of its beauty. Biondo wrote the *Roma instaurata*. The saddest humanist ode on the death of Rome is the work of Poggio Bracciolini *de fortunae varietate urbis Romae et de ruina eiusdem descriptio*, 'On the variation of the fortunes of the city of Rome and on its ruins'. But for Poggio this sadness suggests a scientific interest. In the same way as the consideration of the republican *tabularium* and Vespasian's *lex regia* had given Cola di Rienzo–the Roman revolutionary of the mid-fourteenth century–inspiration for his collection of inscriptions, so now the consideration of the same *tabularium* suggested to Poggio his famous eulogy of the study of inscriptions. But for Poggio, a man of the fifteenth century, the emphasis falls on the greatness of republican Rome, 'when the city', he says, 'was not oppressed by servitude', even though he admits that 'very many and excellent buildings now vanished are remembered' from the imperial epoch. One might call this melancholy of Poggio's the melancholy of the epigraphist, for whom the ancient greatness is revealed in the solemn monumentality of the inscriptions; and, not content with this, he would like to look upon that great expanse of solemn forms of which they speak but which have vanished from sight. The buildings have crumbled as Rome's power has crumbled. Whose is the blame? In this brief work Poggio replies through the mouth of his interlocutor. 'In the giving and the taking back of these things, as of right, fortune is mistress.' Fortune: as in Polybius, in Sallust, and Procopius.

Procopius had been made known in Italy, even before Flavio Biondo wrote his *Historiarum ab inclinatione decades* by a humanist of outstandingly Polybian and Procopian spirit, Leonardo Bruni Aretino. Unfortunately Bruni did not mention the name of the great

Byzantine historian and published his *De Bello Italico adversus Gothos*, which is substantially a reorganization (plagiarism one might say) of Procopius, completed by 1441, as his own work. Procopius's name was given prominence later by Flavio Biondo. But the reviver of Procopius had a profoundly real, contemporary feeling for the problem of the decadence of Rome, or as he called it *vacillatio*, derived from his involvement in humane and political affairs. Procopius had taken 476 as his starting point, though making brief reference to Alaric and Attila. Bruni also realized the importance of 476 but he saw imperial decadence above all as a chapter of Italian history. For him the crises of the barbarian age did not have a catastrophic character; as far as Italian history was concerned life blossomed again out of death. Preparing to narrate the events of what he called 'the Italian war against the Goths' he said: 'While I write these pages, though many things sadden me because of my great love for my fatherland, still one reflexion consoles me; that, if Italy suffered the greatest adversity at that time, she came out at the end victor over the foreigners and remained up to our own times most powerful by land and by sea, and up to this time cities have flourished here which are made splendid by their great riches and are of great authority, and they still flourish, and her glory and empire extends wide and far. So we should not be saddened by the things which happened then but rather rejoice for them. They are like the labours of Hercules; he became more illustrious through them than he would have been without them.'

The end of the western empire appeared to him then as an Italian crisis which went back to 455, precisely to the killing of Valentinian III at Tor Pignattara. 'After the death of Valentinian III who is known to have been killed by his own men, the Western empire began to decline and to become exhausted. There were in Italy at this time very great bands of foreign soldiers, previously called in by Valentinian III against the terror of Attila (the reference is to the descent of Attila into Italy in 462) and then united with the Romans against the Vandals. Seeing this great crisis and the decline of the empire these men took courage and demanded a third part of the fields . . .; the patrician Orestes would not grant the request, the soldiers killed him and, led by Odoacer who had come to Rome, they deposed the Emperor Augustulus [son of Orestes]. Having thus become the masters of the country, they divided a third of the fields amongst themselves. Odoacer, having attained power in this way, governed the city at his whim, in his own name and that of the army.'

Here the date 455 is substituted of course for 475/6, the date which had been given prominence in the first page of Bruni's model, the *Gothic War* of Procopius. 410, the date which strikes the reader of Orosius (it is also important in the first pages [I, ii, 7–30] of the *Vandal War* of Procopius) seems to be forgotten by Bruni. In contrast to Flavio Biondo, for whom 410, mistakenly given as 412, marks the beginning of Roman decadence with the sack by Alaric, Bruni concentrates his attention on the last twenty years of the Empire of the West, as if to emphasize even more what Polybius would have called, if he had known about it, the 'external cause' of the fall of Rome. This apart, Bruni gives as much or perhaps more attention to the 'internal cause', for he has thoroughly absorbed the spirit of Polybius, his favourite author. For him, as for Petrarch and Flavio Biondo, the 'internal cause' is remote. He lays even more stress than Biondo on the importance of the loss of liberty. His formula, as expressed in his *Historiae Florentini populi* ('Histories of the Florentine people') is quite clear: 'the Roman empire began to decay when the name of Caesar, like a ruin, fell upon the city.' For him too imperial government means the elimination of the best people. 'The imperial court welcomed the base rather than the strong, flatterers rather than men of action, and the transference of government into the hands of inferior people brought about little by little the fall of the empire.'

One result of the new understanding of the problem of the Roman crisis was the final downfall of a myth which had already long been attacked from various sides: the Donation of Constantine. Doubts had already been expressed at Rome about the alleged donation in the days of Otto III and again in the twelfth century, but now under the blows of Nicholas Cusanus and above all Lorenzo Valla the old legend collapsed. Lorenzo Valla's little book on *The False Donation of Constantine* was written about 1440. It is not only a demonstration of the falseness of that one document. With the myth of the Donation of Constantine also fell in a sense the myth of Constantine himself; thrown together with the others under condemnation for violence, his reputation could not emerge unscathed from this sort of *bellum diplomaticum*. In an imaginary protest by the senate and the Roman people Valla makes his fictitious orator speak thus:

'. . . You [Constantine] have no rights over the Roman empire. Caesar secured power by force. Augustus imitated him in this stroke and made himself master by destroying the opposing party. Tiberius, Caligula, Claudius, Nero, Galba, Otho, Vitellius, Vespasian and the others made havoc of our liberty by the same or similar means. You yourself have become master by driving out or killing the others. I leave aside the fact that you were not even born in wedlock.'

The criticism of Constantine has thus become an anti-Caesarean critique, and it is also, apart from this, a realistic evaluation of the Romano-barbarian kingdoms.

'If there were cities and peoples (and we know that it happened thus) which, being abandoned by the emperor during the barbarian invasions, had of necessity to give themselves kings, under whom they might defeat the barbarians, should they then have deposed these kings from their thrones? Or should they have reduced their sons to the rank of private citizens even if they were recommended as kings either by paternal tradition or by their own personal bravery? Should they have returned to the Roman empire?'

All this of course implies criticism of the medieval idea of the *translatio*. For Lorenzo Valla the true emperor is the Greek, as he says himself, and the Carolingian empire is only a papal creation. Thus is established a new historical perspective, whose greatest importance is that it follows the concrete juridical and political events.

If the fifteenth century gave us the criticism of the Donation of Constantine, the contribution of the sixteenth century was to criticize the legislation of Justinian. This was the work of the *Culti*, an historical school of jurists who were able, through the discovery of the interpolations in the Codex of Justinian, to show how the late empire voluntarily abandoned the severe lines of classical jurisprudence. The whole great effort of research into Roman law in the sixteenth century, carried out by Budé, Alciati and Cujas was dominated by this problem, whose origin is clearly connected with the French polemic against the universal empire. (This has been given prominence recently by Domenico Maffei.) The scholars' attack was directed against the 'crimes of Tribonianus' (*facinora Triboniani*) and the impact of this scholarly investigation on the interpretation of Roman decadence was enormous. We can find it explained in a conclusive manner in a formula of Antonio Agostino, Bishop of Lerida, the famous humanist jurist.

'The Romans lost their liberty and their empire over the other provinces when they abandoned their ancient customs and institutions, when all the inferior people did not scruple to change the laws. Tacitus speaks well when he says that the Roman state had to suffer first for the sins of the Romans and then for those of their laws and the twelve tables were the last expression of just law. It is better not to speak of Tribonianus against whom all are ready with the charge of corruption, which might be formulated in the manner of Virgil. *Fixit enim leges pretio.* So say the sources; and what is more serious still, he confounded the old and the new and made them over.'

For the man of the Renaissance the *inclinatio* was due to the abandonment of ancient manners, which is in a sense the opposite if what we think today. We prefer to see in the crisis of a society an equilibrium between new requirements and old tradition. But the Renaissance starts from an ancient model which is to be found in tradition itself and the *ordo renascendi* depends on loyalty to this external tradition, almost an immortal phoenix. We all remember the first page of Guicciardini: 'from the time when the Roman Empire, weakened principally by the transformation of ancient customs, began more than a thousand years ago to decline from that greatness to which it had climbed with marvellous virtue and fortune. . . .'

The demoniacal forces which dominated the decline were perceived by Machiavelli[1] in a rhythm of events which leads from ignobility to sloth, from that to disorder and thence to decay and so back to the beginning. He was not the first to formulate a theory of historical cycles. Werner Rolevinck (1425–1502), for example, had spoken of a *cursus temporum*, which we might call the Sallustian cycle, running from abundance to misery to temperance and then over again; and other examples could be quoted. In Machiavelli the series of events is quite different. It is historicized by the interven-

[1] Cf., most recently, Sasso, *Rivista Storica Italiana* (1958), pp. 333 ff.

tion of virtue and fortune, both authors of the greatness of Rome, and the great crisis lies in the disappearance of virtue and the mercenariness of the imperial period. In fact Machiavelli gives a new content to Sallust's motif of decadence as the disappearance of *virtus*, making the caesarism and laziness of the leaders and the faithlessness of the rulers the preconditions of the collapse. The phenomenon of the migration of many peoples, not just one, and of the failure of virtue dominate this most remarkable Renaissance interpretation of the end of the ancient world. For Machiavelli it is almost a matter of pre-ordained and regular migrations, a conception which grafts humanistic motifs onto the tradition of Paul the Deacon.

From another part of Europe, Conrad Peutinger, the editor of Jordanes, set himself the same problem of the migrations of the people. He put forward the image of the *inclinatio* of the empire with the connected *commigrationes exterarum gentium*, *praecipue Germanarum* without any substantial innovation. We meet again in his 'epitome' the motifs of the 'perfidy of Stilicho', who denies Alaric his wages, of Saul 'the Jew', whom Alaric had defeated, of Alaric's burning of Rome, except the Christian churches, placed in 412 instead of 410. A certain prominence is given to the meeting of Attila and Pope Leo. These old, uncorrected errors are however significant, and it may be interesting to notice that Peutinger's epitome also omits the name of Odoacer, which seems to suggest a certain underestimate of the importance of the events of 476. It closes with a solemn statement which is full of Sallustian melancholy: 'So kingdoms die and empires crumble from their foundations and nothing on earth is lasting', *sic regnorum interitus*, *et funditus excisa imperia*, *nihilque in terris perpetuum.*

A friend of Peutinger, Beatus Rhenanus, pointed out meanwhile the national importance of the barbarian migrations from the German point of view. (This led eventually to one very noteworthy result because it made clear the conventional character, for example, of the designation 'Geti' instead of 'Goti' in some sources relating to the Germanic migrations.) Beatus made it a matter of high national pride. 'Forgetful of the Homeric line,' he said, 'according to which, "in our house there is good and evil", we give too much attention to the histories of other peoples, whereas there are on the other hand remarkable deeds of our own, which in some cases may be considered worthy not only to be known but even to be imitated. For the triumphs of the Goths, the Vandals and the Franks are our triumphs. The states set up by these peoples in the splendid Roman provinces and even in Italy and at Rome itself, once the queen of all cities, are a proof of glory for us, even though nowadays there remains only that state founded by the Franks which was always the most fortunate in peace and war. Not that I am an admirer, to speak the truth, of the burning of cities, destruction and the devastation of countrysides, without which victories of this kind are never accomplished, for who indeed who has a heart does not hate such madness? But because we know in general that these things are valued so that all nobility is deduced from them.' Thus the theme of the transition from the ancient to the medieval world came into contact with that of the ethical values which make up 'nobility'. This is the theme which one might call Erasmian.

In 1534 when the Erasmian polemic was at its height Pietro Corsi (Cursius), a member of the Roman clergy, thought to defend Italy against Erasmus, who had denied that the Italians had military gifts. Erasmus replied calmly that, in wishing to praise the military virtue of the Italians, one ran the risk of praising the Goths instead. 'When I was at Rome some scholars seriously held the opinion that the heroic spirits amongst the Italians were descendants of the Goths and the other barbarian nations, whereas the under-sized and ill-born and weak were the true remnants of the Roman race. Whence it was deduced that the greatest part of the Italian nobility took its origin from the barbarian nations.' It has been justly remarked by Renaudet that this passage *expose certaines vues d'une éthnographie fort moderne*. Erasmus has little love for fighting men–one of his favourite emperors was Probus to whom the *Historia Augusta* attributes an essentially anti-militaristic ideal– and certainly he did not aim to insult the Italians in denying their warlike capacity. But the suspicion that the Italian nobility drew its origin from the barbarian destroyers of the Roman empire stands on the same plane of national pride, though restrained and humane, as the attitude of Beatus Rhenanus, for whom the triumphs of the Goths are the national triumphs of his own people.

There is another rather important point. The scholar friends of

Erasmus who made the Italian nobles descendants of the barbarian conquerors were opening a new chapter in historical methodology. For them the problem of the ethnic boundary between the ancient and medieval worlds linked up with a problem which we might describe as heraldic. The end of the aged Roman world and the migrations of the young barbarian forbears of the Italian aristocracy was later, in the eighteenth century, to become a preoccupation of Ludovico Antonio Muratori. The sixteenth century foresaw the possibility of a positive evaluation of the migrations and ultimately of the end of the ancient world in the study of the modern nations; this was the problem for Peutinger and Beatus.

Peutinger and Beatus had met at the 'pan-Germanic' diet of Augsburg. They had a common interest in *res Germanicae*, the study of Germans and Germany, and Beatus was indebted to Peutinger for his copy of Procopius. In the richly animated life of his own Augsburg, the ancient Roman City made German, Peutinger could feel that an eternally recurring pattern of events imposed on states, at a fatal moment, the sleep of death. 'So kingdoms die', he wrote, thinking of the fall of Rome itself. In this too he was a man of his time. The old identification of the fourth empire of Daniel with the Roman Empire, which had dominated the Middle Ages, could certainly still be defeated; the Reformer Melanchthon and the Protestant historian Sleidanus for example were highly authoritative supporters of it. What imperial subject could doubt that Charles V was Caesar in the same manner, almost in the same ideal line, as Augustus, Constantine, Theodosius and Justinian? The Roman empire was there still, in the shape of the empire of the German nation. But, by an extraordinary circumstance, it was also, as the empire of Rome, a distant and completed fact, so much so that Beatus Rhenanus could now speak of the glories of the Germans in antithesis to those of the Romans. The historical phenomenon of the extinct empire was superimposed on that medieval conviction of the eternal empire destined to survive to the end of time.

These two antithetical ideas of the end of the Roman empire in the fifth century and its definition as the fourth monarchy of Daniel continued to exist side by side like adversaries who could not make up their minds to come to blows. They met finally in 1566 when

Jean Bodin, the most celebrated French historian of the sixteenth century, complaining of certain prejudices of his contemporary Calvin, made a fundamental attack on the identification of the Roman empire with the fourth monarchy of Daniel. But behind these celebrated pages in Bodin's *Methodus*, lies the whole Renaissance elaboration of the idea of decadence. The shadow of the dead empire was concentrated on the one year marked by destiny, 412 or 455 or 476. There were other years fateful for other empires as that had been for the empire of Rome.

So the sixteenth century, with its encyclopaedic cultural formation still rooted in astrological traditions, believed that it had reached the moment to uncover this hidden secret of the years of destiny, in which states were transformed and extinguished, by investigating the movements of the earth. In 1505–7 Copernicus had formulated in the *De hypothesibus* his doctrine that the sun and not the earth stood still. In 1540–3 his disciple Rheticus put the new theory in print for the first time and expounded in the *Narratio prima* the Copernican teaching about the vicissitudes of states. 'We see', he said, 'that all monarchies have their beginning when the centre of the eccentric comes to be in a certain notable point of the terrestrial orbit. Thus when the sun's eccentricity was greatest the Roman Empire passed into a monarchical form and, as the eccentricity diminished, so the empire, as it grew older, became less and completely disappeared.'

With this doctrine the Copernican school projected history into the immense space which it had transformed. It was not simply a return to the astrological approach of the medieval chronicler Giovanni Villani. It represented a greater awareness of the phenomenology of the birth and death of human worlds. Rheticus's formula was designed to 'periodize' historical cycles without artificially prolonging the separate duration of governments and states. Jean Bodin subjected it to a concise criticism in his *Methodus*. Bodin did not deny the doctrine of years of destiny, for him too the birth and death of states was deterministically regulated; but he believed the relationship to be not an astronomical but a numerical one based on the perfect number 496. He calculated, with all kinds of distortions, 496 years from the foundation of the Roman republic to Julius Caesar and another 496 for the whole empire from Augustus to Augustulus.

He replaced the astronomical hypothesis of the Copernicans with the old number mystique.

Nowadays these calculations make us smile, though the number mystique, demythologized, has been compared by someone with modern '*statistics of conjuncture*'. But they have their own importance in the history of the idea of decadence. We can certainly marvel that the sixteenth century, the age of Renaissance and Reformation, should have been completely obsessed by astrology and that men like Rheticus and Bodin should have connected historical events with astronomical figures or with multiples of the number seven. Perhaps our very modern view of the system of thought of sixteenth-century man makes us run the risk of misunderstanding this irrational juxtaposition of history and astronomy or arithmetic. We should regard it as only one of the many forms of expression for the need to fit the events called *conversiones*, therefore also the births and deaths of the great states, into a cosmic and universal phenomenology. Therefore for Copernicans as for Bodin the phenomenology of decline appeared in infinitely varied forms. Bodin could speak of the death of Rome as one of many transformations and *conversiones*, beside the *conversiones* of a number of other régimes and states, the Athenian, Spartan, English, Turkish, and so forth. The idea of the four monarchies was thus enlarged and Bodin could proceed to liquidate it. There was an infinite number of forms of decline, represented as if in a panorama by the most diverse combinations. Put beside other 'declines' and the many births and deaths of régimes, the end of the ancient world too became a finite reality, a 'fateful time', which must be investigated through its component parts. It was a fateful time also for Johannes Löwenklav (Leunclavius), a historian who is forgotten today but nevertheless a great one. Löwenklav wrote in 1576 but he transformed the humanist problem of Roman decline into something organic and critically thought out.

6

Constantine, Julian, Justinian: from Löwenklav's 'Apology' to the question of the 'Anekdota'

The new restatement of the problem of the late empire may be said to have been initiated by Löwenklav in 1576 and completed by Gibbon two centuries later: the first a historian whom we have now almost forgotten and the second a historian of universal fame. Though he was a genius, Löwenklav has fallen into relative obscurity. His historical rôle was to be the pioneer of lines of thought which were fully developed much later. Himself a man of the late Renaissance, he opened the way which only the Enlightenment, and in some respects only modern thought, could exploit fully. He has, at any rate, a position of capital importance in the history of European historiography as the first modern interpreter of the end of the ancient world. 382 years after the appearance of his *Apology in Defence of Zosimus* we still feel, as he felt, that the history of the late empire is dominated by the two great contrasting personalities, Constantine the revolutionary and Julian the desperate defender of tradition, and that both must be understood if we are to grasp late Roman civilization in its fullness. Without resorting to the rotation of the earth, like the Copernicans, or to number symbolism, like Jean Bodin, Löwenklav had an equal sense of the drama of ancient

Rome's collapse, of the *tempora fatalia*, as he said, but his sense was that of the pure historian, studying the elements in the situation as they were defined by human nature.

How did Löwenklav arrive at his interpretation of the late Empire? In 1571 he had published an edition of Gregory of Nyssa. In 1576 came the translation of Zosimus with the connected *Apology in Defence of Zosimus*. He had dealt with a Christian and a pagan author within a period of five years. Standing aside from the two opposing faiths which had confronted each other in bitter conflict during the Roman empire, Löwenklav, though he was himself an undoubted Christian, could affirm the need for the most objective investigation. 'Since we have at our disposal', he said, 'historical sources of very different tendencies, the truth will be most successfully sought by the scholar who is capable of judgment and can recognize (through these contrasting sources) the almost living image of the truth.' For this reason his friend Redinger had sought diligently, though unsuccessfully, for the *Histories* of the pagan Eunapius, and for this reason Löwenklav wrote his wonderful *Apology in Defence of Zosimus*. The central problem in the interpretation of the crisis of the ancient world was usually the evaluation of the work of Constantine, but Löwenklav linked this with the interpretation of the antithetical personality, Julian the Apostate, and further with his judgment on Constantius, the Christian, but Arian, emperor, who had given the Caesarship to Julian. In the background was the great question of the connections between the Christianization of the empire and the end of the ancient world; and also an academic debate about the evaluation of the Christian empire in contrast to the principate of the first three centuries. This form of the problem was fully present in Löwenklav's mind and therefore his *Apology in Defence of Zosimus* may be considered as the foundation charter of modern studies on the late empire.

'[The adversaries of Zosimus] say that this historian was hostile to Constantine because Constantine gave the victory to the new religion. So be it; what is to be deduced from this? . . . We should admit that this religious hatred led Zosimus to attribute to Constantine the introduction of that intolerable kind of tribute called *chrysargyron* . . . (the *aurum lustrale* as it is called in books of civil law because it was exacted every five years);[1] we should admit that it was the religious hatred which led Zosimus to accuse Constantine of laying heavy impositions on the property of others. We ought to be suspicious of the Zosimian tradition if it should be established that Zosimus spoke falsely. On the other hand it is possible to demonstrate that Zosimus had good sources for his accusation against Constantine, so much so that, even if the testimonies of others were lacking, Constantine still could not be acquitted of this charge. Even if the tribute of the *chrysargyron* had been already imposed by Constantine's predecessors (which the critics of Zosimus do not dare to affirm) and he had merely maintained it, Zosimus's charge would still in a sense be unaffected because Constantine would not have abolished this hateful tribute already introduced by pagan emperors. In this case then Zosimus did no more than his duty as an objective historian: he reported the matter, as he had learnt it from his sources, honestly. . . . But they admit further that this tax was always fashionable under the Christian empire, from Constantine onwards until Anastasius. . . . Let them cease then to bewail the charge of Zosimus against Constantine. . . . Zosimus says that Constantine was prodigal, once he had gained the throne, because he exhausted the finances of the state with immense donatives, engaged in superfluous luxury expenditure on the largest scale, employed money in a vast number of useless constructions, not distinguishing between prodigality and munificence; all of which is historically accurate, and no one can deny that just for these reasons he must have devised new methods of exacting taxes and introduced onerous tributes since moderate measures were in-

[1] It is significant that Löwenklav, on the basis of Zosimus, grasped the importance of the *chrysargyron* in the economy of the Constantinian state. It was a tax on capital employed in commerce or (if no capital were employed) on commercial activity itself. The concept of 'capital' included for example even beasts used for the transport of goods. Therefore the *chrysargyron* fell indiscriminately upon the whole bourgeoisie and proletariat of the empire from the richest merchant to the innkeeper or the most miserable beggar. The Constantinian state–which for the normal payment of the *annona* to the soldiers always had recourse to direct taxation of landed property (*capitatio-iugatio*, exacted either in kind or in money; *cf. infra*, ch. 10)–found in the *chryargyron* a useful method for the payment of donatives in gold or silver money. Hence the name *chrysargyron*, that is to say 'the (tax in ?) gold-silver'. In emphasizing this question of Constantinian taxation Löwenklav perceived what modern historians call the economic 'planning' introduced by Constantine, or rather perfected by him. (Piganiol, *Scientia* (1947), pp. 95 ff.; *Journal des Savants* (1955), pp. 9 ff.; Lambrechts, *Ant. Class.* (1949), pp. 109 ff.).

sufficient. The essential thing for him was that he should not abandon his policy of abundant issue and granting of money. . . . In the same way we are told that he was liberal with the soldiers, which Zosimus also attests. Nor could he well be otherwise since he had obtained power by means of the army and must persevere in this path, the only one by which he could have made himself preferred to the legitimate sons of Constantius Chlorus, born of the latter's marriage with Theodora. Now all this involved enormous donatives and could not happen without the economic ruin of the subjects. So to report, as does Zosimus, the introduction of this odious taxation and the intolerable exactions carried out by Constantine, or by Valentinian I or Theodosius the Great, is not a denigration of pious and religious princes; it is rather a demonstration of the true facts which may provide useful examples for ourselves. In fact this is a warning to present and future princes that they who protect the Christian religion should not consider themselves authorized to use that arbitrary power against the property of their subjects which Julian and other pagans denied to themselves. Julian and the others were good and moderate administrators and it would be shameful if our Christian princes were to be surpassed in this by pagans. . . . If then Zosimus recognized objectively some glories and merits of Constantine this confirms that he was certainly a good historian; . . . you others however, who attack Zosimus for so little, do not make gods of the Christian princes, or anyway do not exalt them to the skies with praise. . . . Certainly Constantine was great in name and deed. Who denies it? . . . But it is the duty of those who would narrate the events of Constantine's age to record not only the praiseworthy things about him but also those which are otherwise; the law of history demands it. . . . Even some of those who, unlike the pagan Zosimus, follow our religion, do not hesitate to attack Constantine freely. . . . They attack him for the change which came about in his old age when, at the suggestion of his sister Constantia he recalled Arius, the author of a most immoral heresy, from exile and had Athanasius deported to Trier. . . . Evagrius and Nicephorus attack Constantine because they say that Crispus Caesar, a youth of outstanding virtue [the son of Constantine] and Fausta Augusta [Constantine's wife] were killed by Constantine himself. . . . They say that no mention is made of these murders of Constantine by Eusebius Pamphyli, a contemporary who survived Constantine. But I prefer Zosimus to Eusebius. It is a mistake to resort to witnesses like Eusebius and in general to historians like him. Eusebius did not want to present Crispus as guilty because everyone knew that he was not, and on the other hand, so as not to accuse Constantine, he avoided saying that Crispus had been killed by his father. . . . From this one may fairly deduce that Crispus was truly innocent, just as Zosimus relates, saying that the grandmother of Crispus, Helena, unreservedly condemned the crime. Therefore Eusebius, for his own reasons, preferred to take up a neutral position, while Zosimus, being further removed from the time of these events, could speak the truth and indeed could not avoid doing so. And I marvel that these same historians, not content with making such absurd observations against Zosimus, also want to deny all cruelty in Constantius II. . . . Certainly Gregory of Nazianzus, the most severe of men, praises him for hatred of Julian; but Julian was in reality, on account of many great virtues, not only equal but superior to Constantius. . . .

'There is yet another charge against Zosimus, by which he would be, according to his critics, guilty partly of lying and partly of insulting Constantine. Zosimus says that Constantine, tormented by remorse for his violated oaths and murders and other crimes, and failing to find purification in the religion of the pagans, passed under the inspiration of a Spaniard called Egizius to the Christian teaching for the sake of the serenity of spirit which it offers to the penitent who appeal with confidence to the Son of God, the reconciler of men with God. The critics of Zosimus deny this. They exclude the possibility that Constantine might have committed the said murder and observe in opposition to Zosimus that Constantine obtained at the end of his life that purification from sins which is achieved through baptism. But this removes nothing from the truth of Zosimus's account. In fact Constantine could still be a follower of the Christian religion even if he obtained baptism so late. In those days it was the custom that the followers of Christianity should delay baptism until the last years of their life because, I suppose, they believed (as indeed some still believe now) that with baptism our life is purified from every sin and it is not necessary, once this has been obtained, to expiate in any other way.'

Here we have the prototype of the problem of Constantine as it always appears in modern historiography: the problem of the personality of Constantine, of his violence, his conversion, made so much more obscure by his baptism almost at the point of death; furthermore the problem of the economic policy of extensive issue of money introduced by Constantine, profoundly different in its results from the policies which were followed by his nephew Julian, who was so tragically akin and so tragically opposite to him. (With the statement of this economic problem Löwenklav foreshadows historiographical tendencies of very recent times.) Above all certain illusions disappear from the myth of Constantine and, almost in antithesis, there arises the myth of Julian which, two centuries later, will be the centre of Gibbon's historical experience. In the face of this great innovation no one will want to waste time on Löwenklav's trivial error in transforming the 'Egyptian come from Spain' of whom Zosimus speaks into 'a Spaniard called Egizius'. Even the pragmatic style of these evaluations (one must not forget that for the humanist history is normally the *magistra vitae*) takes nothing from the historiographical importance of the Constantine-Julian antithesis as pointed out by Löwenklav.

'Let us leave religion on one side', says Löwenklav, 'and see what kind of a man Julian was. In Julian there were, not merely suggested but apparent, multifarious signs of outstanding virtue; so much so that if they had not been obscured by his error in regard to the worship of the true God it would certainly have been permissible to see in him the ideal embodiment of the good prince, and even when he was very young. . . . Who then, I ask, however hostile he may be to Julian would not wish to exalt this illustrious man for so many admirable virtues of spirit and of body? . . . Yet there are writers so devoid of all spirit of humanity that they do not hesitate to belittle his virtues solely on account of his apostasy and to declare him to have been an unfortunate or even ruinous prince for his state. The reason they give is that he was not successful in the Persian war and that being killed in enemy territory, he brought enormous harm upon the state. The truth is different. Those two nations which were so dangerous and fateful for the Roman empire, the German and the Persian, were reduced by him to such difficulties that one was defeated in grievous battles and urgently sought and obtained peace, which it carefully preserved although it was always by nature warlike and impatient of peace; the other, terrified by this continuous series of victories confessed, however unwillingly, that it had been close to final ruin. . . . All the fear and harm on this account ought, on the contrary, to be attributed to his successor Jovian, a man of our religion. In fact, Jovian, to the eternal shame of the Roman name, made himself almost a suppliant to the victorious enemy, and while the Persians (who were spontaneously seeking peace) should have ceded part of their territory, he actually appeased them by the cession of numerous provinces.'

Löwenklav's exaltation of Julian foreshadowed certain motifs in Gibbon: the talent, the temperance, the generous spirit, the chastity of Julian. It was founded, amongst other things, on the works of Julian himself. It had as an inevitable result the re-examination of the pagan view, also stated by Zosimus, that the crisis of the Roman empire had been due to the abandonment of the ancient religion. It is natural that Zosimus's Byzantine critics, against whom Löwenklav reacted, should have opposed this pagan attitude with as much violence as it had been opposed earlier, in a western world under attack from the Goths and Vandals, by the great Bishop of Hippo, Augustine. But the Augustinian solution existed within the sphere of metahistorical reflection about the crises of the earthly city. Augustine had not ventured to make a strictly political comparison between pagan and Christian emperors. Such a confrontation became possible only in the Byzantine world and it had led to the paradoxical conclusion of the critics of Zosimus, who had stood the pagan thesis on its head and attributed to the Christian empire political successes (concretely expressed in terms of power) positively superior to the victories and conquests of pagan Rome.

Löwenklav was aware of the gravity of the new problem. Since he denied, as seemed to him necessary from the standpoint of historical 'objectivity', the superiority of the Christian over the pagan emperors, he ran the risk of returning to the old pagan thesis of Christianity as the cause of the death of Rome. His Christian convictions ruled out such a solution. 'The causes of the fall of Rome', he concluded, 'are to be studied otherwise, requiring that one should investigate the reasons for which these sad fallings of kingdoms and confusions and massacres occur at certain fatal moments of history (*fatalibus quibusdam temporum momentis*) . . . history teaches us that this happened often in times past and in the full light of our own times. We see it happen daily.' Removed from the ancient dispute between pagans and Christians–that is between traditionalists and revolutionaries–the question 'why did the ancient world die?' remained essentially unanswerable; or rather it was reduced to the consideration of the decisive moments (the *fatalia quaedam temporum momenta* of Löwenklav) in which history overthrows kingdoms and massacres men.

Löwenklav had before him the example of his own times. When he was writing in 1576 spirits were subdued, in spite of Lepanto, by the Turkish menace. His whole life as a student and, one might say, as a politician, was dominated by the encounter with the Turkish world. He had discovered the text of Zosimus during an embassy to the Turks and he was the founder, with his *Historiae musulmanae Turcorum*, of the modern study of Turkish civilization. The great fear which Islam had excited in Christendom for nine centuries remained a standard of comparison for the fatal period in which the ancient world fell. Later there will be other *Ideen* which can similarly call forth a new vision of the late empire and of the migration of peoples; in the second half of the eighteenth century, two hundred years after Löwenklav, will come Herder's vision of the 'inundations' and 'rejuvenation' of future centuries by the peoples of the Ukraine and Russia and the Steppes of central Asia. The road by which history may attain 'objectivity' lies through the pressure of contemporary preoccupations. Though this may seem a paradox it is a truth confirmed by experience and indeed comprehensible *a priori*.

In the first half of the seventeenth century one man who was immersed in the contemporary life of his own time and yet fascinated by the great historical problem was Hugo Grotius. His tolerant Protestantism suggested to him a Christian vision of the history of Europe–'Europe' is a word which appears frequently in the thought of the men of this time, confronted by the terrible wars of religion. In his famous little book *On the Truth of the Christian Religion* (*De veritate religionis Christianae*), which appeared in 1639 we find, among other things, an exaltation of the religious life of the Christians in the first three centuries, a motif which implicitly suggested the conception of a 'secularized' Christianity in the late empire. In 1640 appeared his commentary on the biblical texts relating to Antichrist (*Commentatio ad loca quaedam quae de Antichristo agunt aut agere putantur*). With an intuition which has been confirmed by modern studies, he traced the early Christians' idea of Antichrist to the horror which the madness of Caligula had inspired during the early empire and, above all, he saw in the Revelation of St. John a true and proper prophecy of the barbarian migrations, or more strictly, of the 'rebellion of the *federati* against the empire which', he said, 'began in the age of Honorius'. (Note the periodization in the manner of Flavio Biondo.) Thus in the eyes of a fervent Christian the end of the ancient world appeared to be conditioned, in accordance with the Orosian tradition, by the symbolic significance of a divine sanction. But Grotius's chief contribution to the study of the Roman crisis is not to be found of course in these two little works of apologetics and exegesis. His great intellectual battle was concerned essentially with the very modern idea (though it had some Senecan and Tacitean roots) of the noble savage. Grotius was above all the student of natural law and his thought was always dominated by the primitivist aspiration towards spontaneity and simplicity in law. Therefore the old criticism of the *Culti* directed against Justinian's law and the *facinora Triboniani* became for him a revaluation of the contribution made by the barbarians, men of simple and just laws, to the juridical structure of Europe. In the *Prolegomena*, admiration for the Gothic world, which had become a professional interest (he was Swedish ambassador in France in the decade 1634–45), made him regard the Goths and other barbarians as builders of a simple and sane society on the ruins of a corrupt world.

Naturally the exaltation of the Germans, which we have already found, if in a limited form, in Beatus Rhenanus, was not a great novelty, least of all in Swedish tradition, which had always regarded the Gothic glories as a matter of national history–if the Goths had come from Sweden the real fount and motherland of Germanic virtues was always there. The Swede Joannes Magnus, last but one of the Catholic bishops of Uppsala (the last was his brother Olaf) had written a *Gothorum Sueonumque historia*, published posthumously in 1554 by his brother. Modelling his work on the *Decades* of Flavio Biondo, the Swedish bishop had insisted that 'the *inclinatio* of the

Roman empire had its origin with the Goths', but, in contrast to Flavio, he had traced the fall of the empire to the terrible crisis of the third century, more precisely to the *Gallieni inertia*, 'the incapacity of Gallienus'. In general the *Historia* of Joannes Magnus, with its ingenuousness and its sonorously nationalistic tone, was a feeble and monotonous work–all the virtues belonged to the Goths and as usual Alaric was deceived by the *ingens perfidia* of Stilicho. Nevertheless the history of the Goths, seen as Swedish national history, could open up interesting new points of view on the fortunes of the Roman empire, already tested by the barbarian invasions of the third century, in what we would call the age of Commodian. The epoch of Gustavus Vasa (King of Sweden 1523–60) gave a new impulse to the Germanic pride of the descendants of the ancient *Suiones*, just as marked in the Lutheran statesman Gustavus as in the Catholic historian Joannes Magnus. About a century after this awakening, Grotius, whom we may call a Dutchman turned Swede, saw again in his Goths the ancient sons of the Scandinavian country which had given him a noble mission in life. In his new historical perspective Salvian, Isidore and Jordanes seemed to speak with a more elevated voice as stern judges of Roman decadence and ardent investigators of the barbarian spirit. Even the old motif (which appeared already in Erasmus) of the Germanic origin of the neo-Latin aristocracies, revived by Grotius, acquired almost a tone of humane austerity. It was fitted into that kind of *elogium* of the migration of the peoples which seemed to distort history by throwing over the old empire of Rome the shadow of its guilty exhaustion.

'The harvest of Gothic, Vandal and Lombard laws will not be accepted by those who admire only Roman things. I see in Roman laws an ingenuity which seeks out trifles, an instability and inconstancy, and in the end so great a mass, such uncertainty, that no one can have a memory so good that he will not stumble often in those contradictory laws. My philosophy wishes that the law should be simple, brief, clear, like, for example, the government of fathers over their families. The constancy of such a law carries with it much authority and I am happy to find this in the laws of our Northerners. Therefore I think that if this simplicity had not pleased God as much as the subtleties, he would never have given its majestic strength to the laws of these innocent peoples. Usage (no false judge) amongst many peoples, prefers these (Germanic) laws to the Roman: Sidonius tells us that in Gaul the laws of Theodoric, not those of Theodosius were in force. . . . (However let us make a comparison, by the chief divisions, between Roman and Germanic law).[1] . . . In public law there is the same fundamental structure of laws, depending amongst the Romans on the will of the prince; that is of one man who may easily be mistaken or change his opinion. Therefore among so many imperial edicts one conflicts with another. Justinian not only changed many at the bidding of that Tribonianus who was altogether corrupt, he furthermore changed his own opinion on the same matter three or four times. Amongst your (Germanic) peoples, on the other hand the laws, properly moderated by the princes and by those elected by the orders of the people, have three advantages: because of the number of good councillors the laws cannot conceal anything harmful, they are observed with pleasure because they are derived from common agreement, they are never changed except by absolute necessity. . . .'

This exaltation by Grotius of pure Germanic customs has then its own innocent national prejudice. It has also however, conceived as it was in the age in which Alemanni published the *Anekdota* of Procopius, a methodological interest. For Grotius it is a 'Procopian' problem, but regarded from a religiously tolerant standpoint (therefore he sees in Procopius's Christianity something rather like his own Christianity, anxious for unity, withdrawn from the conflicts between opposing confessions), and he strains to emphasize the anti-Justinianian, pro-Germanic aspects of Procopius's work. In vindicat-

[1] Grotius's doctrine of the superiority of the Germanic laws to Roman law led to difficulties of which Grotius himself was aware. How does one explain that Justinian, to whom we owe the famous *Codex* of 529, had defeated the Vandals in 533 and the Goths in 535–555? Grotius replies that to preserve the purity of their virtue the Vandals and Goths would have had to avoid the frequent marriages with the defeated Romans and to convert the occupied lands into common lands (a provision which he praised in the state of the Incas and also in the primitive Roman state). Grotius's primitivism thus connects the problem of the barbarian migrations in the Roman Empire with that of the Indian policy of the Spanish *Conquistadores* who had become by chance the ideal heirs of the migration of peoples. In any case the importance of Grotius's *Prolegomena* for the history of civilization is worth noting. Grotius pointed out amongst other things the affinity between the Germanic languages and Persian. This discovery, though derived from a mistaken equation of Scythians with Goths, foreshadows Bopp. Today it is forgotten. But Grotius was aware of the importance of his discovery, writing about it, for example, to Schmaltz in terms which betray his justified pride.

ing the purity of the ancient Goths, which seemed to him to be attested by some passages in Procopius, Grotius declared that doubts of the sincerity of the professed Christianity of the historian of Caesarea were without foundation; and thus he took up a position on the question of the Procopian *Anekdota* (or as they were and are commonly called the *Secret History*) which, in the seventeenth century, was undoubtedly the most vexed and discussed work in late-Roman literature.

This debate had been opened by the librarian of the Vatican, Nicola Alemanni, who had discovered the work and published it in 1623. Alemanni, who came from Ancona and was of Greek ancestry, was initiated into the study of ecclesiastical history in the tradition started by Cardinal Baronio with the *Annali*, published between 1588 and 1607. Baronio's tradition could not have very much sympathy with Justinian. Preoccupied with safeguarding Egypt at all costs, this great emperor had tried to reconcile orthodoxy with the rebels against the Council of Chalcedon and therefore had to keep up a conflict, sometimes bitter and sometimes restrained, with the popes. The discovery of the *Anekdota* seemed a blessing to the historians of Baronio's persuasion. Now at last a new aspect of Justinian had come to light, the ruler dominated by the demoniacal Theodora. And in fact Alemanni was in a sense a minor Löwenklav. Just as the tradition of Zosimus had led Löwenklav to demolish the myth of Constantine, so the new work of Procopius led Alemanni to a revision of judgment on the personality of Justinian. The discoveries of new texts are in some ways less accidental than they seem at first sight; there is generally something 'necessary' in the meeting between the searcher and his discovery.

Though the methodological importance of the criticism of Constantine may be compared with that of the criticism of Justinian, the nature and results of Alemanni's revision were however far removed from the spirit which had enlivened the great pages of Löwenklav. Löwenklav had aimed to liberate the historiography of the late empire from sectarian preoccupations. Through his criticism of Eusebius and Gregory he had given students a new understanding of the relationship between the figures of Constantine and Julian, which is essential to the history of the fourth century, and his discovery had been something altogether new and original. Alemanni's criticism of Justinian's personality, on the other hand, was a kind of seventeenth-century pendant to the glorious criticism of Justinian's legislation, which had been carried out in the sixteenth century, in connection with the discovery of the interpolations. It was not therefore altogether new. But it appeared as such because by now the criticism of the *facinora Triboniani*, which had arisen in France as an expression of the new French science of law, was falling into the background.

The essential question was modern. The problem which excited the polemic about Procopius was the relation between church and state. To Alemanni and the 'Baronians' in general Justinian appeared as an enemy of the papacy. To the jurists who opposed Alemanni, Justinian appeared as the defender of the rights of the state. Thus an apparently strange situation arose: the jurists, who in the sixteenth century had made unceasing attacks on Justinian and the *facinora Triboniani*, now became the inflexible supporters of Justinian against the *Anekdota* of Procopius and against Alemanni. Not Grotius however. He defended the rights of the state, not by reference to Justinian, but with his Ostrogoths, and moreover his religious tolerance prevented him from thinking too clearly in sectarian terms. Though he was an extremely devout, but not fanatical, Lutheran, Grotius succeeded in winning the love of the Catholics, and after his death Father Petan said the mass for his soul.

The opponents of the Procopian *Anekdota* and of Alemanni were of another temper. They would certainly never have understood the moderation of Grotius, the uncertainties of Schmaltz, or the conversion of Queen Christina. The most determined of them was Joannes Eichel, jurist to the house of Brunswick. When he attempted to confute Alemanni in 1654 he put into his writing the intransigence which had inspired the Brunswick family in the Thirty Years War and the anxiety which shrinks from compromise. (Mazarin was preparing the League of the Rhine.) Justinian appeared to them in the guise of their own lords and also of the Great Elector Frederick William. The charges made by the *Anekdota* seemed to them so absurd that Procopius could not have been their author. . . . And what of the rights of the critic? Is it impossible to touch the great men, the heroes? 'Naturally', said Eichel, 'I am not ignorant of the *Apology* of Löwenklav in defence of Zosimus; but I am so far from considering it, except for a small part, decisive that I would certainly maintain on the contrary that it has demonstrated the absolute impossibility of defending Zosimus. It is as clear as daylight that in those days writers like Zosimus were common enough and no one will be so malicious or wretched as to give the slightest credence to the charges of Zosimus against Constantine'. For Eichel, Löwenklav's criticism of Constantine, based on Zosimus, was absurd and Alemanni's criticism of Justinian was equally absurd in the same way.

This was, in part at least, a step backwards. Today no one doubts the authenticity of the Procopian *Anekdota* and naturally no one would think of throwing away such an important source. The modern historian knows very well that he has no right to put himself in the position of judge or confessor to condemn or absolve and he knows equally well that all the voices of an epoch have the right to be heard, even when they are directed against the great myths or question the stature of the giants. The history of the late empire is a story of tragic and powerful men, Constantine, Julian and Justinian amongst them. Löwenklav had shown that the way to understand them was to place oneself at a suitable distance from them all so as to catch the contrast between the various voices. In spite of Eichel's attachment to the great traditional myths, this approach was repeatedly rediscovered every time that research overcame the instinctive practical preoccupations of the moment and became capable of grasping the dimensions of the conflicts–often paradoxical conflicts–at the end of a world. It was significant of these conflicts that the tradition of the great Justinian had to struggle, after an irreversible inversion of values, with the Procopian idea that Justinian was the prince of demons.

The era which stretched from Löwenklav to the Procopian controversy was then in a sense the most profitable for the establishment of a critical historiography of the late empire. The comparison of interpretations transmitted in the best-known texts with interpretations completely opposed and almost unsuspected hitherto–Eusebius with Zosimus, the *Wars* of Procopius with the same author's *Anekdota*–brought to light that complex interweaving of diverse elements and evaluations which is the true pattern of every great historical event. And, since the appearance of the late empire changes according to one's interpretation, for example, of Constantine or Julian the Apostate or Justinian, one may say that the presuppositions were being discovered for a real scientific historiography which deals with the shadows beside the places of illumination. In the years 1626–52 Godefroy could write a remarkable commentary on the *Codex Theodosianus* which is still today a valuable administrative history of the late Roman empire. Every modern library in which the end of the ancient world is studied includes amongst its most important reference works this book by Godefroy, and from the late seventeenth century, the work of Tillemont, from the eighteenth century Montesquieu's little essay and Gibbon's monumental *History*, beside the works of Sybel, Dahn and Seeck from the nineteenth century and Stein and Piganiol from the twentieth. There is no break in the continuity of scholarship from Godefroy and Tillemont to our own day. Of course the spirit of men changes: 'their' sense of decadence was conditioned by the rise of religious disputes within the framework of the religious confessions and then, in the eighteenth century, by the definition of the principles whose abandonment determined the crisis. Our idea of decadence in the nineteenth century and after has a larger pathological element and sometimes seems to resemble the expectation of Antichrist in the Roman empire itself and the Middle Ages. But many of the problems which we extract from that distant past, a millennium and a half away from us today, are 'their' own problems. Was Constantine converted? In what sense was Julian opposed to him? How did Christianity triumph over the classical world? Why was the unitary economy of the Roman empire broken up? Did the barbarian flood break into a world which was already crashing? . . . The same questions were on the agenda of the historians eight or ten generations ago. The seventeenth century sensed them and sometimes posed them; the eighteenth century certainly posed them. We can now examine them one by one, the ways in which they were stated and their dialectical changes, as they have developed from that time to the present day.

PART TWO

7

The Religious Problem

It has recently been suggested[1] that Eusebius, the famous biographer and contemporary of Constantine, was responsible for the distinction between the ecclesiastical and the political history of the Roman imperial period; and that therefore we, who regard the study of the one kind of history separately from the other as plainly impossible, have to correct an error which originated essentially in the age of Constantine itself. But, in this instance at any rate, Eusebius seems to be quite innocent. He did indeed write an *Ecclesiastical History*, following the remarkable example already set in the second century by Hegesippus, but it is not true that he was trying to isolate the vicissitudes of the Christian communities from the general framework of imperial history when he described them in that book. Of course this does not necessarily mean that he was a great historian, only that he is not responsible for the distinction between the two kinds of history.

Bolingbroke, in his *Letters*, made the opposite charge against Eusebius, that he had 'corrupted the waters', confusing sacred and profane history. The truth is that the late empire and the Middle Ages, in applying, with varying completeness, the kind of explanation which is provided by the idea of 'divine judgments', put profane history at the service of ecclesiastical history. It was ecclesiastical

[1] Cf. W. Weber, *Kaisergeschichte und Kirchengeschichte* (1929).

history, as sacred history, which gave the key to the understanding of human events. (In fact Walafrid Strabo, the most gifted historian of the Carolingian period, and perhaps of the whole Middle Ages in the west, made genuine discoveries about the conversion of the Germans to Arianism.) The Humanist-Renaissance epoch discovered profane history and thus the distinction arose. But, from Löwenklav to Godefroy and Grotius, the need to overcome it became ever clearer, and the point of departure was the personality who dominates the final phase of the ancient world and who was so much discussed by Löwenklav: Constantine.

One could now study critically the traditional 'vision' and with it the conversion of Constantine. Godefroy, a lawyer, debated the authenticity of Eusebius's *Life of Constantine*. Oisel, the numismatist, thought Eusebius's whole account of Constantine's vision a fairy tale. In 1679 appeared the second of the *Libri Miscellaneorum* of Etienne Baluze[1] the librarian of the Colbertine, which contained a decisive vindication of the traditional Eusebian account. 'And what will there be left to call true', said Baluze, 'if we can relegate to the category of ancient inventions a story like this which is based on the testimony of Lactantius, Optatus, Porphyry, Eusebius, and also of coins? Matters like this should be treated with more piety and that irreligious temerity should be far removed from Christian souls.' Baluze's protest against the 'irreligious temerity' which had made the Constantinian question possible certainly seems out of place in our eyes nowadays, but it is an interesting piece of evidence of the obstacles which were encountered in the late seventeenth century if one tried to break down the barriers between ecclesiastical and secular history.

The barriers were broken down by a Protestant pastor, Le Sueur. He is a forgotten historian now, but between 1672 and 1677 he published a *Histoire de L'Eglise et de L'Empire*. Of course he attached enormous importance to the age of Constantine. 'We have seen the usefulness of joining the history of the empire with that of the church for the period from the first to the third centuries; for the centuries which follow this method appears quite essential, in as much as the most notable actions of the emperors were those things which they did in favour of the Christian Church or against it.

[1] Cf. Mollat, *Dictionnaire d'Histoire et de Géographie Ecclésiastique*, VI, pp. 439 ff.

Therefore we consider it necessary to unite them.' The idea of decadence and 'corruption', as he said, had then an important place in his work; but it was above all an idea of religious and moral decadence.

'By these things (riches, luxury and so on) one may see how the purity of the Christian religion was insensibly affected. . . . We ought principally to consider what great strides the Arian heresy has made in the century through the assaults of false teachers and the protection of emperors and empresses. . . . Another important factor is the dissipation of a large part of the Roman empire, a dissipation which was the work of the barbarians who flooded into it and increased the barbarism, ignorance and superstition. . . . We enter the fifth century, full of strange calamities. In the fourth century God had sustained good emperors who gave peace and well-being to the Church. But, since the Christians had abused it and turned it into dissolution, giving themselves up to vices, the Sovereign Judge of the Universe was angered by their rebellion and made them feel just afflictions, especially the afflictions of a terrible war. The foreign and barbarian nations burst into the Roman empire like a flood and broke it into pieces so that each powerful leader had a part of it in which he could establish a separate kingdom. Thus may be seen in this century the beginning of the fulfilment of the prophecy of Daniel and that of St. John in the Book of Revelations: that ten kings, that is to say more kings or kingdoms, would have to arise on the ruins of the fourth empire which is that of Rome. During those terrible moments the Church suffered much. The Prince of Darkness made ignorance, superstition and errors arise in various forms.'

In spite of this vision, which is greatly affected by the idea of decadence, Le Sueur regarded the history of the emperors with a sort of benevolence. Some of them had even aided 'the advances of the Faith'. He had, in particular, no reservations about Constantine, no doubts about his vision and conversion, and he applied to the problem of his delayed baptism the correct explanation which had already been given by Löwenklav. He also tried to give an objective judgment on Julian, regarding him as a man of talent.

'If this ruler had been Christian and God-fearing, he would undoubtedly have deserved great praise and would have shown good qualities in the government of the empire. He was keen, chaste, sober, patiently hard-working, a protector of scholars, wise and eloquent. Nevertheless even Ammianus Marcellinus, a pagan, speaks of him as a frivolous man, rather talkative and superstitious. In truth people of this kind deceive those who place trust in them.'

Le Sueur's judgment on Stilicho, who had been severely condemned by the Orosian tradition, was inspired by his desire to escape from the Orosian pattern and was decidedly contradictory. On the one hand he attributed to Stilicho *conseils et ordres salutaires*; on the other he condemned him for *méchantes actions* and *malheureux desseins* for the last period of his life. But the earthquake of 408 seemed to him a presage of evil rather than (as it had seemed to Baronio) almost a protest by the forces of nature against Stilicho's betrayal. Justinian received great eulogies, expressing in fact Eichel's point of view rather than Alemanni's. Thus the first modern historical work which assumed the necessity of uniting the history of the Church and the history of the empire applied the concept of 'corruption' and the corresponding medieval category of 'judgments of God' with the aim of achieving a relative balance.

The idea of the corruption of Christianity in the fourth century which was emphasized, amongst other things, in the *Historia Ecclesiastica* of Spanheim (*luxus gliscens in Ecclesiam*) did not yet extend to a complete condemnation. But this came soon after from the pietistic tradition and its classic expression was in the famous *Impartial History of the Churches and the Heretics*,[1] published by Gottfried Arnold and completed in 1688, to which Goethe owed his interpretation of Christianity. Constantine, who had been discussed by Löwenklav more than a century earlier on the basis of historical considerations, was now condemned by Arnold because of an evaluation by religious criteria.

In speaking of 'religious decadence' Arnold seemed to be taking up a concept which had been used from the earliest times of Protestant historiography, the concept of a 'fall' or 'estrangement' from original Christian purity. But, in this pietistic writer who sympathises with the heretics, this Lutheran concept takes on an uncompromising form which involves Constantine and the whole late

[1] On Arnold cf. now Meinhold, *Saeculum* (1950), pp. 196 ff.; Hirsch, *Geschichte der neueren protestantischer Theologie*, II (1951), pp. 260 ff.; and the classic pages of Meinecke, *Entstehung des Historismus*, second edition (1946).

empire in a religious and also political condemnation. The uniting of the two sides of history, the great requirement at the end of the seventeenth century, led to a renewed application of the Orosian category of judgments of God, but in a completely different form, for Orosius had in fact exalted Constantine. It was now exposed to the various gradations of sectarian attitudes or simply, in the case of Arnold, to the strictness of the *collegium pietatis*.

The Abbé Tillemont[1] also wished to unite the two histories. Originally his *Mémoires* for ecclesiastical history were part of his *Histoire des Empereurs*, and only fear of censure led him to separate them. Just because he placed his enormous learning at the service of the 'liaison' between the two sides of history, he created a work of scholarship which remains fundamental. The profane part, the *Histoire des Empereurs*, began to be published from 1690 on, the *Mémoires* from 1694. Eighteen and twenty two years respectively had passed since the publication of Le Sueur's *Histoire de L'Eglise et de L'Empire*. Tillemont's work certainly reflects that Augustinian spirit which inspired the whole of the production of the age of Louis XIV, bridging sectarian divisions and infusing the *Histoire* of the Protestant Le Sueur, the great *Discours* of the Orthodox Bossuet, the work of the Jansenist Tillemont and the *Histoire Ecclésiastique* (published from 1691 on) by the Gallican Fleury. But Tillemont was capable, for example, of understanding, and giving positive value to, the 'objectivity' of the pagan Ammianus Marcellinus. To see to what extent he could resist the Orosian tradition, one may consider, as we did in the case of Le Sueur, his treatment of the individual who was Orosius's bête noire, Stilicho, the effective ruler of the western part of the empire in the decisive years from 395 to 408.

Tillemont managed to show that, in spite of the hostility of a part of the work of the pagan Zosimus, Stilicho had on the whole a good press from the pagans, while the Christians delivered an inflexible judgment of condemnation on him. This observation did not enable him however to go on to an historical judgment. He confined himself to confronting the exaltation which the pagan Claudian gave to Stilicho with the hostility of Orosius, and he accepted in full the Orosian idea of the different judgments of God (he said 'Divine

[1] On Tillemont cf. Momigliano, *Rivista Storica Italiana* (1936), p. 4 ff.; *idem*, *Contributo alla storia degli studi classici* (1955), pp. 107 ff.

Providence') expressed in Stilicho's victory at Fiesole–which therefore appeared to him, as to Orosius, a miracle–and in the final success of Alaric. He did not of course grasp the extreme conflict between tradition and religious revolution which made the drama of the age of Stilicho, or rather, to be more precise, this conflict was for him the inescapable divergence between sources inspired by the two opposed faiths. Nevertheless this was a notable step forward if one thinks that these sources are in the final analysis the direct voice with which the age of Stilicho speaks to us, the age in which lived not only St. Augustine, St. Jerome and Orosius but also Claudian. The voice is indeed confused and complicated by conflicts: on the one hand pagan traditionalism in its period of eclipse, which no longer had ears to listen seriously to its intransigent and victorious enemies–Claudian confined himself to a formal adherence to Christianity, writing a hymn *On the Saviour*[1]–on the other hand those intransigent, modern men, men like Augustine, Jerome and Orosius, who regarded Claudian as a 'most obstinate pagan' and found Stilicho's protection of this damned soul disturbing and offensive. Out and out Augustinians, as the writers of the age of Louis XIV were, found it difficult to keep aloof from the violent conflict in which their party was clearly placed and committed. It is enough that Tillemont should have felt and understood the significance and origin of the opposition between the sources.

This conflict went through the whole history of the empire from the time when ancient man began to lose the assurance of his old spiritual inheritance. Above all it is at the root of the fourth century division which was summed up for Hrosvitha and Löwenklav, and is summed up for us, in the antithesis between Constantine and Julian. Of course Tillemont had no doubts about the vision and conversion of Augustine. When the French period of Augustinian historians, the age of Louis XIV, was well in the past, all seemed ready for a more detached interpretation in entirely human terms. This was the interpretation of Gibbon[2] whose *History of the Decline and Fall of the Roman Empire* began to appear in 1776. It grew out of a polemical inspiration; the friars were singing Vespers in the

[1] Schmid, *Reallexikan für Antike und Christentum*, VII (1955), pp. 152 ff.

[2] Giarrizzo, *Edward Gibbon e la cultura inglese del settecento* (1954); Momigliano, *Historia* (1954), pp. 450 ff.

Temple of Jupiter at Rome. This is a reversal of the medieval interpretation of Hrosvitha or Hildebert. It is also a reassertion of the need to study both the gradual victory of Christianity and the gradual crisis of the ancient world in their relationship with each other on the plane of human history.

Gibbon declared that he wished to write history without prejudice. Tillemont had had no doubts about the vision and conversion of Constantine, and Fleury had found it necessary to believe Eusebius and Zosimus at the same time–an impossible reconciliation as Löwenklav had already shown–but for Gibbon the key to Constantine's soul was his ambition, the foundation of the Christian empire was the product of his genius as a politician. Just for that reason, however, Constantine's great revolution seemed to him to be linked with the spiritual power, the 'five causes' by which he explained the victory of Christianity over the pagan empire. This spiritual force, in his judgment, expressed itself above all in the powerful organization of the Church, the 'fifth cause', which a man like Constantine could not resist turning to account. And, since the best proof of the organizational power of Christianity was to be found in its resistance to the persecutions and in its relation to new ideals–zeal, the virtues, faith in miracles–so the problem of Constantine was propounded by Gibbon as a corollary to the problem of the persecutions, and the sections relating to the persecutions were interpolated into his treatment of Constantine.

One hundred and eighty years later this connection between the problem of the persecutions and the problem of Constantine still seems to us unquestionable and necessary, though entirely new demands may draw us away from the solutions offered by Gibbon. His interpretation of Constantine as a wise politician, in whom virtues and vices were mingled, was to have a great future. In the late Romantic period it was developed and deepened by Burckhardt, whose work of genius *The Age of Constantine* was published in 1852–3. In this book too Constantine's religious sense seems diminished or denied and replaced by his political intelligence, which enabled him to grasp the importance of Christianity as a universal force. Even Burckhardt's thesis of the 'demonization of paganism' is foreshadowed in some pages of Gibbon. Again, Gibbon's interpretation of the persecutions starts from the idea of Roman tolerance of foreign religions, and thus the nineteenth century raised the question of their juridical basis, envisaging with Mommsen the hypothesis that they were police action (in as much as the admission of Christianity involved the abandonment of traditional religion), or the doctrine that they were the application of an *institutum Neronianum*, or some other possibility. Thus, in the two basic questions of Constantine and the persecutions, the point of departure was always essentially Gibbon's statement, through the re-thinking and revision attempted in the work of great modern historians–Burckhardt, Renan, Mommsen, Seeck and Duchesne–and in the problem of the 'Hellenization of Christianity' (Harnack). Some scholars still uphold today the interpretation of Constantine as a pure politician; others however insist on his religious sense and the decisive importance of his conversion. Some, in dealing with the persecutions, speak of a 'small number of martyrs', a thesis dear to Gibbon and to Dodwell before him; others insist on the traditional interpretation. Recently an interesting debate, provoked by Grégoire, has reconsidered Gibbon's theory.[1]

To deepen our understanding of this problem as far as is possible today, we have to approach more closely the troubled sensibility of an age that witnessed the collapse of the values of classical culture, which had once been universally recognized. We must understand the discordant harmony of the voices which move between the pagan world and the Christian revolution. A cold political calculation is not really enough to awaken in a man, even a great man, the energy required to change the face of the world. For this reason Constantine cannot be considered a pure politician. He certainly believed in the God of the Christians and his delayed baptism must be explained not as an expression of religious indifference, but, on the contrary, by his hope of a complete purification, as Löwenklav already realized. His conversion is only the point of climax in the conversion of a whole world. To understand the conversion of Constantine involves indeed studying the whole epoch which it ended, the epoch of the persecutions, as Gibbon had grasped. It

[1] Recent works on the persecutions are Grégoire, *Les Persécutions dans l'Empire Romaine* (1951); Sherwin-White, *Journal of Theological Studies* (1952), pp. 199 ff.; Vogt and Last, *Reallexikon für Antike und Christentum*, pp. 1159 ff.; Schmid, *Maia* (1955), pp. 5 ff.; Moreau, *La Persécution du Christianisme* (1956); cf. Vogt, *Historia* (1957), pp. 508 ff.

must be studied with a realization of the contradictions which are peculiar to the great periods of decline.

For this reason it is worth going back into the history of the empire. For the historiography of our time the problem involves, above all, the interpretation of the second and third centuries. One might say that the spiritual change which leads from the old world to the new has its most interesting manifestations, and in some ways its most lively expression, in the age of Commodus and the Severi from 180 to 235. This age of *temps houleux*[1] witnessed a typical divorce, so to speak, between the law, which regarded Christianity as a crime, and the spiritual reality which already knew the first notable examples of Christian art and the very finest of Christian inscriptions, the famous inscription of Abercius. The official persecution of the Christian was accompanied on the other hand by an enormous diffusion of the new religion in the eastern parts of the empire and the adhesion to it of no less a person than Marcia, the very powerful concubine of the emperor Commodus. There is an insoluble contradiction between the classical tradition, which is formally untouchable, and the spiritual revolution, which has already corroded and weakened it on every side. It is just this contradiction which is protracted for a whole century up to Constantine, the emperor who believes in the God of the Christians and who, seated at the Council of Nicaea on a golden throne, modestly declares himself to be bishop only over the laity.

The fascination of the age of Commodus and the Severi lies then in the contradiction which pervades it. There is no period in the whole history of our civilization which is as rich as this in paradoxical absurdities. About 184–8, during the reign of Commodus, Callistus, a banker slave, who will one day be Pope, is accused and condemned for the crime of Christianity. Everyone knows that he and his patron, the powerful imperial freedman Carpophorus, are both Christians, yet, when Callistus is accused of Christianity, Carpophorus himself makes every effort to defend him and hastens to declare that Callistus is *not* a Christian. Only the strong and obstinate faith of Callistus, who gives the lie to his patron, determines his condemnation to forced labour, and the courageous slave ends up in

[1] The famous expression of Huysmans, *A Rebours*, 44.

the mines of Sardinia. The thoroughly Christian bishop Hippolytus, a rigorous man, when telling us of these events constantly gives Carpophorus the attribute *pistos*, which means Christian. Carpophorus's weakness was not enough to make him lose his place in the Christian community. Even a Christian like Carpophorus then acknowledges officially that Christianity is a crime and therefore tries to exculpate his slave; a very significant contradiction indeed.

In the eyes of all the Roman emperors, even those closest to it, Christianity remained officially a crime. Its criminal character followed from the fact that the Christian was, by his very *nomen* of *Christianus*, a declared follower of Christ, who had suffered under Tiberius a sentence of death at the hands of the Roman state. At the same time, writings of Christians are read and published everywhere, *didaskaleia* of Christians are found everywhere, the names of Christian bishops are known, and the properties which they administer, and so on. There is officially a crime of Christianity yet Marcia, the lady who rules the court and the heart of the Emperor Commodus, is a Christian or close to the Christians (*philotheos*), even according to Hippolytus. There is a Christian rigorism, of which Hippolytus is the expression, and yet the Christian work *de Aleatoribus* perhaps by Pope Victor, tells us of Christians who do reverence to the God of the pagans while they play dice.

Under Commodus, who reigned from 180 to 192, we find famous cases of persecution, yet a Christian text which is contemporary with him tells us that the reign of this emperor is not only a period of peace for the empire but also a period of peace for the Christians. Or again: everyone knows that the Manes are pagan and yet you can find the inscription *Dis Manibus* on the funeral tablets of Christians. Septimius Severus (193–211) confirms the rescripts of his predecessors against Christianity, yet Tertullian in 212 will present him as *Christianorum memor* and his son as *lacte Christiano educatus*. Sextus Julius Africanus, to whom Alexander Severus entrusted the direction of a pagan temple, the Pantheon, is nevertheless a Christian, but he uses pagan magic formulas. Men live two lives, one lazily settled in tradition, the other more or less decisively revolutionary in spirit and in fact Christian. The classical historians who are contemporary with Commodus and the Severi do not tell us about Christianity, though this is the religion dear to Marcia and holds undisputed sway over the great masses of Asia Minor and Syria. For a man like Dio Cassius, Christianity, which he never explicitly mentions, is only one form of 'Judaic customs', yet this historian came from Bithynia, a region which had ceased to honour pagan gods more than a century before his time. Tradition compels these members of the pagan aristocracy to ignore this phenomenon, characteristic of their crumbling society, though their wives go to Christian *didaskaleia* and they themselves are forever seeking contacts with the bishops. But reality always revenges itself on abstract forms. Imperial rescripts against the crime of Christianity are always valid but they are not in practice easy to enforce. They can be enforced against the courageous slave Callistus, but never against his powerful and prudent patron Carpophorus.

The Christians were the great creative minority and the history of the new age was woven by their new construction. The concepts of minority and majority are indeed relative. Already at the time of Trajan whole regions in the east were no longer pagan. But a world which had produced Homer and Virgil and Roman Law resisted the abandonment of the forms of its civilization even if they had already been emptied of substance. This produces the contradictions of the age of the Severi, then, a century later those of the age of Constantine and finally those of the age of Stilicho.

Already towards the end of the first century A.D. many pagans had sensed that their world was beginning to give way. But they would not surrender. At the same time, about A.D. 100, Plutarch observed that the oracle of Delphi was declining and he put forward demonological explanations of this 'decadence' far removed from reality. Yet in his dialogue *On the Eclipse of the Oracles*, some of the speakers look for real 'causes'. One of these, a cynic, says that men have become too wicked, another says that they have become too few in the classical land of Greece. Is this a kind of 'elimination of the best'?

8

Marriage in late Roman Society

The concept of the 'elimination of the best' is commonly linked with the work and personality of a great historian of the late nineteenth century, Otto Seeck. But it is not, or not in all respects at any rate, an invention of Seeck. One could even defend the view that it is implicit in any theory of *inclinatio*, as the humanists called it; implicit in the sense that an *inclinatio* or decline, an abandonment of the highest, or archetypal, forms of culture, presupposes the spiritual exhaustion of the old world which had developed those forms. As early as the Carolingian period Dungal thought that the *voluntas* of ancient man was superior 'because of the youth of the world and the strength of body and vigour of the senses'. The idea is to be found in embryonic form especially in the humanistic period. It seemed to Petrarch that, as if through the influence of some unlucky stars, heaven was against the men of his time. Flavio Biondo deduced the *inclinatio* of the Roman empire from a degradation of imperial Roman society, which constantly strengthened the ignoble people obedient to the monarch instead of the free and courageous spirits. In explanations of this kind the loss of liberty becomes decadence because it coincides with a moral phenomenon, which in its turn is connected with the 'passing away' of personalities and of 'graceful spirits'. But Flavio Biondo would never have emphasized such a passing away except for a pure moral evaluation, nor would it have been possible to do this before the nineteenth century. For the eighteenth century the idea of decadence is especially bound up with the disappearance of 'manners' and likewise of 'maxims' and 'principles', not yet of men, still less of the corresponding vitality of these men.

Only the nineteenth century, with its largely voluntaristic and vitalistic attitude, could introduce, one might say without realizing it, a kind of biological aspect into the general idea of decadence. In some of its expressions it introduced into modern culture that idea of the 'old age' of states and men which had been expressed in the Roman world, with an implicit exaltation of liberty, considered as an attribute of youth, by Seneca the Elder. Through Florus it had come to Christian thinkers like Cyprian who employed it to show that decadence was not due to Christianity but was just an ordinary biological phenomenon, necessary and irreversible because it coincided with the end of the world. The romantics of course substituted for the 'end of the world' the end of the 'Latin peoples', tired and almost gasping for breath, like the French after the Revolution in Chateaubriand's *Mémoires d'outre tombe*. Soon the idea of senescence began to be identified with that of the decadence of peoples and, as the end of the ancient world is a paradigm for every interpretation of decadence, it inspired a masterpiece of late Romantic historiography, Burckhardt's *Age of Constantine*, which we have already mentioned and which appeared in 1852–3. 'The whole history of this time', said Burckhardt, 'is nothing but a clear testimony of the senility and decadence of Roman life, for which things no blame is to be attached to Christianity.'

Amongst Burckhardt's observations in Chapter 7 of his book one might select three, all very penetrating but very debatable and at the same time characteristic, for evaluating the concept of decadence in the world of this born historian: the consideration of the 'silence of the rhetoricians about the empire'; the judgment 'on deformity and physical degeneration' at least in the upper classes; and the idea of 'degeneracy in fashion'.

Criticism of these concepts is not difficult. One can say that if the sophists of the imperial period are silent about the empire, preferring to exalt personalities and subjects from the Greek and republican periods, it is because their interests are inspired by a humanistic ideal and they are encouraged by their training to evoke the period of ancient liberty and therefore to contrast 'the kingly man' with 'the tyrannical man'. In fact the cultivated and traditionalist classes in the empire classed as a 'tyrant' not only a Domitian or a Commodus but also Alexander the Great (thus for example Aelian who lived in the age of the Severi) and, especially in the third century, reacted against the militarism of the empire and against the fiscal policy and inflation. Thus the opposition of the sophists illustrates *their sense* of decadence rather than *an aspect* of decadence, and an age which contains humanistic manifestations of this kind cannot be, as such, an age of degeneracy; it is, if anything, an age in which the classical values appeared more real than ever and in which a tragic conflict arose between tradition and modern times. Moreover a German historian, Johannes Straub, has recently (1939) demonstrated that the formulae of the rhetoricians of the imperial period have a genuine propaganda significance and that they introduce us to the charismatic conception of the empire, so that their harking-back to the ancient models does not prevent, for example, the exaltation of the divine mission of the modern period, in which the ruler is precisely ruler by the grace of God. (Straub has rightly emphasized in this connection the importance of a passage in the rhetorician Themistius.) As for the deformity and physical degeneracy of which Burckhardt spoke, one has to point out that the sculptured monuments (today one would think immediately of the mosaics of the Piazza Armerina) convey to us just that anxiety of troubled inner life, which was expressing itself in the new religious sensibility and in the spiritual revolution by which classical transformed itself into Christian civilization. The 'possessed' or, later, hieratic faces of the late empire convey to us not a sense of physical decadence but one of spiritual tension. And finally, fashion. Here the longing for luxury, which Burckhardt underlined, has to be considered in conjunction with the assimilation, which was not at all luxurious, of barbarian habits, such as the use of trousers, which was derived from the riding dress of the steppes. Here again there is a revolution in taste, which is consistent with the usual conflict between tradition and the new reality. At Rome in fact the emperors forbade people to go about in trousers or other such barbarian clothes.

Nevertheless these three observations by Burckhardt, two of

which come up again in Seeck, have an unquestionable importance. When he was writing his *Constantine*, European culture was in between the old romanticism and the new positivism. In France the second empire posed agonising problems. In 1868 Prévost-Paradol was insisting on the 'signs of decadence' of the Latins as opposed to the Germanic powers. These were, in particular, demographic signs; the French birthrate seemed to him to be discouraging. Thus appeared again the Polybian image of the crisis of Greece conquered first by Macedonia and then by Rome. According to Polybius the conclusive aspect of this crisis had been the *oliganthropia*, the decline of the birthrate. People like Prévost-Paradol were inclined to ask themselves whether Prussia had undertaken in Europe the task which Philip's Macedon had carried out, according to Droysen's reconstruction, in Greece. The Franco-Prussian war of 1870 deeply affected the historians of the two opposite sides. The manifesto of Von Sybel brought a reply from the great French historian Taine. Von Sybel was for that generation the learned interpreter of the barbarian invasions and of the death of Rome under the weight of Germanic kingship: his *Rise of German Kingship* is a classic. Taine, an anti-Romantic positivist, and yet a strongly romantic man at heart, had always contrasted healthy epochs and sick epochs. Before and after the 'débâcle' he insisted on the idea of decadence occurring through the destruction of the historically creative classes. The idea of 'the elimination of the best' was in the air.

The novel idea which Otto Seeck wanted to introduce, and which was expressed precisely in the formula 'elimination of the best', was meant to involve an exact examination of the family and the sociological conditions which had brought about the end of the Roman empire through demographic decay and the disappearance of the best men. This was the central problem of the famous first two volumes of his *History of the Decline of the Ancient World*, especially of the first, published in 1894 and soon republished in a second edition in 1897. Seeck belonged to the generation which was completely dominated by the problem of heredity and natural selection. The book of books for this generation was Darwin's *Descent of Man*, and Ribot's *L'Hérédité* and other similar books all followed in its wake. For this generation the great question (which has been taken up again recently, though with other presuppositions, in the Soviet Union) was how to determine the forms and characters in which the laws of heredity were manifested–for example the Spencerian transmission of acquired characteristics. And the second problem was the influence of customs and conceptions of life on the 'blossoming and ageing' of peoples–in 1889 appeared a book by Georg Hansen about this blossoming and ageing which, like the works of Darwin and Ribot, had a great influence on the thought of Seeck. Thus, and especially in this second way, the eighteenth-century idea of the corrupted 'manners' of the Roman empire, abandoned without regrets because of its plainly moralizing tone, returned unobserved through the back door in books bristling with figures and biological notations.

Seeck brought something vital to the positivistic atmosphere which had developed in this way: confidence in his power to explain the end of antiquity by careful investigation of the everyday life, even the family life, of that classical world which called itself the empire of the Romans. Because of the previously unhoped-for concreteness which he brought to the subject, every theory about the late empire evolved by a modern historian has to take account of Otto Seeck's work and is a debate, even if an armed debate, with the master. The two points in his analysis which are still famous, and seemed central to him also, are his examination, or rather perhaps his condemnation, of Roman marriage, and his theory of natural selection in reverse. We can begin our debate with the first point. Seeck's theory about Roman marriage goes back to the republican and Augustan ages.

'When, in 131 B.C., the censor Metellus preached against celibacy, he used, among others, the following argument: "If we, o Quirites, had some way of living without wives, none of us would wish to take on himself the trouble of marriage, but, since nature has willed that one cannot live without wives, even if life with them is not entirely satisfactory, a man must take care of his permanent salvation rather than of his momentary convenience." Every Roman would have subscribed enthusiastically to Metellus's words. In fact a century later, Augustus read this speech in the senate and brought it to the notice of everyone by public display. Two centuries after Augustus a rhetorician exercised his powers in criticizing the speech and wondered whether it would not have been better if the censor had painted the advantages of marriage in bright colours rather than making his appeal merely to nature. The rhetorician however came to the conclusion that the disadvantages of marriage were indeed too well known to all men and that Metellus had been right to speak in this way since extenuations and subtleties would have been quite useless. Whereas nowadays (1894), at least in Germany and England, almost every love story ends with union in marriage and thus marriage comes to be acknowledged as the crown of human felicity, for the Romans it was on the contrary a necessary evil and nothing more.

'This difference in points of view is closely connected with another . . . Children were often married at the age of nine or ten . . . the tender and pure feelings of our betrothed couples were quite unknown to the Roman. When the young wife began to reveal to her husband her feminine charm she had already lost for him the charm of first acquaintance. Marriages for love could occur only in the case of widows or of divorced women and, even in these cases, they were unusual, so that it was considered simply ridiculous to fall in love with one's own wife. "Any love for the wife of another man is to be disapproved," says Seneca, "but exaggerated love for one's own wife is also deplorable. . . ." With attitudes of this kind . . . marriage became a mere transaction, in which the dowry played the decisive part. No doubt this is not a characteristic confined to the Romans and the Greeks. In primitive conditions this type of marriage occurs amongst all peoples and even today our peasants marry in the same way. Moreover one cannot say that these marriages must necessarily be unhappy. The more primitive a people is and the more spiritually unawakened a class is–so that the difference between individuals in it is less developed–the easier it will be to put together married couples arbitrarily without their life together causing too troublesome antipathies. . . . But the Roman world had already advanced beyond this primitive stage of civilization, without, however, outgrowing the form of marriage custom which is appropriate to primitive societies. The personality of the cultivated Roman, by now clearly defined, had certain requirements but no one pretended that they were satisfied by an adequate marriage. . . .'

By drawing attention to Roman marriages within the framework of the imperial crisis the master posed a fundamental problem. Recent investigations by the French historian Marcel Durry,[1] amongst other things, have confirmed the existence of marriages arranged when the woman was still a young child. In the sphere of law this is connected with the extent of *patria potestas*. But Seeck did not solve the whole problem. We must analyse the question itself for ourselves; and we have to try an approach to which Seeck did not pay sufficient attention: that is to 'historicize' the question completely. Let us put the question in this way: was the arranged marriage, that spectre which is supposed to have marked Roman houses with an inescapable sentence of tedium or even simply of death, always, throughout the imperial epoch, the unquestioned controller of Roman married life? We have to question the upper classes on whom, according to Seeck, the spectre bore more heavily than on the others. The women of senatorial families in the ruling class attract the attention of the historian. Their marriages, their ambitions, their passions, in short the style of their life, under the curious gaze of all Rome, and often the world, really had enormous importance. One might say that the history of the senatorial order–that is of the upper class *par excellence*–was also the history of the daughters and wives of the senators. The result of our investigation is an interpretation which it would be reasonable to regard as exactly opposite to Seeck's.

One premise is necessary. Of the two ruling classes of the Roman empire before Constantine, that is to say the senatorial class and the equestrian or knightly class, the senatorial has one unmistakable characteristic which is important for its family life. These great lords with aristocratic and famous names transmitted their title of rank, *clarissimus*, to their womenfolk, daughters or wives. The women therefore come to be called, in the definitive systematization of titles, *clarissimae feminae*, 'honourable ladies'. But not the knights. These important gentlemen, faultlessly dressed in togas with narrow purple stripes (while the senators had broad stripes),[2] proud of their right

[1] Durry, *Comptes rendus de l'Académie des Inscriptions et Belles-Lettres* (1955), p. 84; *Gymnasium* (1956), p. 187.

[2] It does not follow that at the height of the empire senatorial ladies were able to wear these clothes, which distinguished their fathers or husbands from the equestrians. But in the late empire a case of this kind may occur. The heiress of a senator who dies

to wear the golden ring, could not give their daughters and wives their titles of rank, which were finally defined as *egregius*, *eminentissimus* and *perfectissimus*. There were indeed knights who wielded enormous power; one has only to think of the pretorian prefects (the commanders of the imperial guard) and the governors of Egypt, when they were drawn from the equestrian order. Moreover the equestrian order, the backbone of the great empire's bureaucracy, enjoyed that unconditional authority which is always reserved for the aristocracy of wealth. But the *dignitas* of the senatorial order was very much superior. Even in the early empire, the fathers of senatorial families bounded by this pride of caste, made their daughters marry within the sphere of the senatorial order. And it was natural that this *dignitas* should have an extraordinary power over the women too. They were born with the rank of senatorial ladies and they attached importance to retaining it. But the rigidification of Roman law led to the establishment at the end of a very hard rule; if the senatorial lady, *clarissima*, had married an equestrian or, worse still, a plebeian, she ceased to have this rank.

The period of the Roman empire before Constantine lasted more than three hundred years, the first three centuries of the Christian era. The senatorial women of this period had inherited in a sense the ethical ideals which characterized the home-bound 'spinning women' and completely faithful wives (*lanificae*, *univirae*) of the best republican period, those splendid and terrible Lucretias and Cornelias who continued to be the patterns of virtue. Otto Seeck would also of course have acknowledged the existence of such virtues, except that, to him, they would perhaps have seemed too classical and official. We may grant that he is more or less right about this, with the reservation, however, that we must remember the senatorial lady celebrated in the so-called *Laudatio Turiae*, who

without having been able to fulfil the obligations deriving from his election as praetor assumes the obligations of her father in proportion to her inheritance. Thus she becomes, though in a secondary way and only in part, 'praetor'; she assumes the sumptuous senatorial dress. In the late empire when the old equestrian class (which we might call the upper middle class of knights) had in fact disappeared, the senatorial *dignitas* was on the other hand higher than ever. In admitting that even a woman could adopt senatorial dress the old class with all its *dignitas* was giving way on the one hand to certain 'feminist' tendencies and on the other, more particularly, to the economic difficulties (because it was difficult to find a person willing to undertake the heavy burden of the praetorship with its responsibility for very expensive games).

saved her husband's life, and the fact that the *Laudatio Turiae* is not the only text of this kind. However, in spite of our modern depreciation of the eighteenth-century 'history of manners', the crisis of virtues has a meaning, and in the early period of the Roman empire many of those Lucretias and Cornelias had come down from their stiff thrones, and they had come down too much. So let us look at some authentic dramas from that age which the textbooks call 'Augustan' and 'Julio-Claudian', dramas which came out of the inner sanctuaries of the senatorial families–of which there were about 600 to 900 in the imperial period–and passed on to the city squares and into the theatres and thus into the books of the historians.

One famous story is that of Augustus's unfortunate daughter, Julia–naturally, as the emperor is a senator his daughter is a lady of senatorial rank. But there are others, less well-known but not less significant. For instance, there is the story of a lady called Aemilia Lepida, a niece of the famous triumvir and also a descendant of Sulla and Pompey. She had already been divorced by Quirinius twenty years earlier, and was now being prosecuted by him on various charges, amongst others for having questioned astrologers about the fortunes of the house of Tiberius, when she betook herself to the theatre of Pompey to lament publicly amongst a crowd of other matrons the obscurity of the origins of her ex-husband, who, although he was a senator, had forbears rather less illustrious than his wife's patrician ancestors. Or there is the opposite kind of story of another Aemilia Lepida, who fell in love with a slave and, being discovered, avoided trial by means of suicide. The period in which these two ladies lived was the earliest period of the empire, under Tiberius, successor to Augustus. A profound insecurity, the legacy of the civil wars, made the lives of some aristocrats and the lives of their women and their marriages particularly complicated.

The early imperial period is a time of feminism and of freedmen. New formulas are being sought and the old state finds itself faced by revolutionary spiritual realities. One important change which has already appeared is that, while good senators in command of armies and provinces march mechanically along the traditional paths, their wives, as if compelled by anxiety, are questioning the priests of oriental religions. There are two outstanding cases: Paulina under

Tiberius and Pomponia Graecina under Nero. Much less notable but still significant is the case of the senatorial lady who marries outside the senatorial order: one recalls Poppaea who married as her first husband the commander of the Pretorians–therefore an equestrian, though in this case he had also received senatorial honours. The Julio-Claudian and the Flavian periods are followed by the age of the humanistic empire of the second century. In appearance at least, the family life of the aristocracy is less troubled at this time. An example is the virtuous Calpurnia, praised by her husband the famous senator Pliny, panegyrist of Trajan. She hid behind a curtain to listen to the intellectual work of her husband, who was no longer young. The third century however sees a return of the feminist tendencies and the power of the freedmen which had characterized the early empire. The oriental religions had enormous success amongst the senatorial ladies (*clarissimae feminae*), beginning with the empress Julia Domna, daughter of the priest of Elagabal of Emesa. Some Christian senatorial ladies found difficulties in marrying within the ambit of the senatorial order where they would inevitably find husbands who, as proconsuls or *legati* or urban prefects, would pronounce heavy judgments against their co-religionists. When they were married they interceded for the accused Christians with their husbands, and some were successful; but Christianity remained a crime and the ruler had to condemn it. Others preferred to assert their own initiative in the choice of a husband, thus breaking up the mummified traditions of family law and risking the loss, if their husbands were not senators, of the title of *clarissima femina*, to which they were not unnaturally attached. This is just the point which enables us to reverse Seeck's thesis.

Seeck thought that the crisis of the ancient world, on the path which led from the principate to the late empire, was marked by forced marriages. The opposite is the truth, for it was just in the period of the later empire, from the time of Marcus Aurelius and still more from that of the Severi, that the rebellion against tradition took place. His diagnosis of the Roman aristocracy as being without love-matches appears inadequate precisely when one considers this later period which he pitilessly condemned. In the brilliant houses where the senatorial ladies of the third century lived we find couples who pose new problems to a pathologically traditionalist world. Soaemias, niece of Julia Domna, marries an equestrian. She *ought* therefore to lose her senatorial rank, but the emperor who loves too this passionate and courageous Syrian, elevates her lucky husband to the senatorial order. Mammaea, another niece of Julia Domna, having married a senator, makes a second marriage with an equestrian. She too therefore ought to lose her senatorial rank; but, by one of those concessions which the emperors make only 'in very rare cases', she is allowed to keep the senatorial *dignitas* which, legally, she ought to have laid aside.[1]

These are marriages of senatorial ladies, but of the imperial house. More significant are other cases of ordinary senatorial women. As early as the reign of Marcus Aurelius some of these would like to marry freedmen, that is emancipated slaves. The philosopher emperor, a proud defender of ancient tradition, declares then that the marriages of senatorial ladies (*clarissimae*) with freedmen are legally null and void. The emperor's reaction tells us a great deal. We can understand the social significance of the marriage of a senatorial lady with a freedman. If Marcus Aurelius had not intervened with his threat of nullity, this matron, with her aura of aristocratic dignity, respected by everyone, would have been able to marry even a slave. She had only to manumit him or, if he was someone else's slave, to secure his manumission. But it is rather significant that these ladies should have had such intentions. One must remember that in marrying a freedman they would not only have lost the senatorial *dignitas*, which was the aim of highest ambition in the Roman-ruling class, they would also have aroused something like a feeling of disgust in the whole of the society which had seen their birth. If Marcus Aurelius thought it necessary to prevent scandal with a precise enactment, this means that he felt the gravity of the threat. He certainly thought that unquestioned traditions ran the risk of crumbling if even a few of these mad women had succeeded in their

[1] Mammaea's second husband remained an equestrian (*minoris dignitatis vir*: Ulp. *Dig.*, I, 9, 12); unlike the husband of Soaemias (Dio. LXXVIII, 30, 2–3) he was not *adlectus* to the senate (Barbieri, *Albo senatorio* (1952), p. 65, n. 264–5, mistakenly includes him in the roll of senators); thus already under Caracalla the principle was affirmed that though it was quite an exceptional matter, a senatorial lady could retain her rank even if she married a man of inferior *dignitas*. This principle was then extended by Soaemias to all senatorial ladies through the institution of the 'little senate of ladies' under Elagabalus, as we shall soon see.

object. And indeed these mad women, daughters of senators who wanted to become wives of ex-slaves, showed a courage which one might say is unheard of in the society of our own time, which Seeck held in such high esteem. (So do we, it is understood, but with some discretion.) We must underline the word 'marry': they wanted to marry manumitted slaves.

Our conclusion is that the state of mind of senatorial ladies of the imperial period was rather far-removed from what Seeck supposes. They were beginning to believe in themselves, not just in their virtues. In the age of the Severi we find a genuine feminism, developed and bold. Here again we must remember Soaemias, the Syrian of great beauty who was represented as Aphrodite and adored as Hera. After she had become first lady of the empire (the emperor was her son Elagabalus, the fourteenth priest of Elagabal) she arranged the setting up of a 'little senate of ladies' with its seat on the Quirinal. One source, the *Historia Augusta*, describes the duties of this 'little senate' as being to issue decrees on the relations of high society among senatorial ladies. The same source gives us one rather more interesting detail: the 'little senate' was connected with an institution concerned with providing *ne innobilitatae manerent*, that is, 'to prevent the loss of nobility by senatorial ladies who had married non-senators'.

This particular expression, word for word, is very noteworthy. Here in fact is a formula completely analogous to another which is used in the Christian camp for the transmission of an edict of Pope Callistus, who directed the community at Rome at the same time as Soaemias was Augusta. Pope Callistus, according to his contemporary and opponent Hippolytus, authorized *de facto* unions, of senatorial women with men of whatever rank–including, then, freedmen or slaves– in such a way that the ladies, by such unions, 'should not lose their nobility'. This is the same age (214–17; 214–18) and the same problem, though of course the feminist solution envisaged by the Empress Soaemias through the 'little senate of ladies' is on a rather different plane from that proposed by Callistus, the ex-slave become Pope. The father's consent was necessary for the marriage to be legally valid, and for those women who did not marry senators, there was a danger of losing senatorial rank; yet the senatorial ladies had in the 'little senate' or in the edict of Pope Callistus, means of defending their autonomy of choice according to their feelings. In this way too the third century sees the dusk of ancient pagan civilization. The old tradition of privilege is breaking up. Inscriptions of the third century also make known cases of senatorial ladies who kept their rank though married to non-senators, or even to ordinary plebeians–typical are those of the Christians Hydria Tertulla and Cassia Faretria. Meanwhile, on the Quirinal, the 'little senate of ladies' revived by the Emperor Aurelian (270–5) carried on the 'parliamentary' feminism of the time of Soaemias.

Our juxtaposition of the formula used in connection with the 'little senate of ladies' (*ne innobilitatae manerent*) and the analogous formula of the edict of Pope Callistus shows us the seriousness of the disturbance which gave women a new consciousness and gave Roman marriage a new aspect. In this case too it was the Christian spiritual revolution. Persecuted by the law as a crime, Christianity affected from top to bottom the society which resisted it, which was defeated and continued to resist. It entered the home and taught women to marry the husband of their choice, if possible a co-religionist, and that in any case they must attempt to convert him. The teaching of St. Paul was authoritative. In houses where there was a Christian woman the relations between the two sexes were transformed. Families in which the women, as Seeck says, served only to give legitimate descendants to the father, were succeeded by families in which the women, with their initiative and their faith, struck severe blows against classical tradition. Seeck saw only the first kind of family and missed the second. But it is from the second that the modern world substantially is derived and it is in this sense the complete reversal of the Greco-Roman world. The modern exaltation of women and of love has its origin here, in the cultural ferment of the later Roman empire, though it has been filtered through the chivalrous emotions of the new protagonists of post-classical history, the Germanic peoples.

Though they had had a Catullus, the classical peoples would never have understood, creators though they were of the finest poetry in the history of the world, the enormous importance of romantic love in modern art from Tristan and Iseult to Madame Bovary. But the men of the third century could perhaps have understood it in a sense, and still more the men of the late empire, among whom the Christian women had a great importance. (The life of Julian the Apostate as a child was saved by his mother's religious friends.) The last pagan senators, who resisted fiercely even after the foundation of the Christian empire, were themselves possessed by a kind of mystical warm-heartedness. We know no poetry of married love which is more human and moving than the lines inscribed on the tomb of Vettius Agorius Praetestatus, a pagan senator of the age of Theodosius, and his sad widow. 'I would have been happy, o my husband, if the gods had granted me that you might survive me; but yet I am happy because I am yours, and was yours, and soon, after death, shall be again.'

Our debate with the master, Otto Seeck, may thus be regarded as closed so far as it concerns his deductions from the unhappiness of Roman marriages. What we have said about the senatorial women, the representatives of the upper classes to which Seeck was especially referring, must in fact be true also for the lower classes, for which Seeck himself allowed a greater possibility of well-matched marriages. From our point of view we can also add that in the lower classes, where they must have been very numerous, Christian women would have had considerable opportunities for converting their husbands. These men were not obliged to respect official tradition, as were the senatorial rulers and the equestrian bureaucrats. Moreover the women of lower social strata were often more fertile in initiative. The Christian empire was created by Constantine, the talented son of a stablewoman, who had managed to conquer the heart of Constantius Chlorus. The problem of domestic life, regarded from the point of view of the Christian spiritual revolution, also has in this case some quite special aspects.

What then determined the demographic decline of the late empire? Since, unlike Seeck, we cannot now point to the system of arranged marriages, we must once again consider this same spiritual revolution which emancipated women from subjection to a paternalistic traditionalism. The nearer to the end of the world people thought themselves to be, the more rarely, in the ruling classes, they raised the families of ten sons for which there is still evidence in the late second century. The same women who had brought about that spiritual revolution accepted willingly Eusebius's admonition according to which, as the end of everything drew near, people should not think of having a son or two to guarantee their physical posterity but should rather ensure spiritual descendants to themselves through evangelization. The lower classes, burdened by taxation, could easily accept that admonition. Here again, if we remove of course the idea of the imminent end, we are at the origins of modern civilization. There is a great difference between these wives of the late empire and the good wife of the affectionate Xenophon. They make one think of Claudel.

It would however be a mistake to suppose that the Eusebian ideal of making an end with *paidopoiia* and *polyanthropia*, carried very great weight in the demographic crisis. The depopulation was rather more serious in the west than in the east and in the countryside than in the cities. If the Christians had carried out Eusebius's recommendations to the letter, we should have to expect the opposite situation; the east should have had the greatest decline in the birth rate. In this case again the real crisis was not only demographic, so to speak, in origin. With the exception of the plagues which raged terribly through the whole empire in the times of Marcus Aurelius and Commodus, the Gallic provinces were depopulated because the peasants could not manage to support the weight of the tributes. They gave themselves up to *latrocinia* (the brigand Maternus was famous as early as the age of Commodus) and enrolled in bands of partisans (the *Bagaudae*). Unlike the Gallo-Roman middle class and aristocracy, which with Rutilius sang the last great song of the dying empire, a great many Celtic peasants, who for a long time did not give up their own language, offered a strong resistance to Romanization. The same is true of Pannonia, Africa, Syria and Egypt. Gaul was the first to fall in the great invasion of 406; it was the creation of Caesar and the heart of the west. Syria and Egypt, the creations of Pompey and Octavian, fell at the first touch of Islam in the seventh century.

These considerations also contain an implicit destruction of the other point in Seeck's theory; that the best men had disappeared by means of natural selection in reverse. If one means by the best men, as Seeck did, the scions of the aristocracies of an earlier period, their disappearance need not matter very much. Great evils often came from the nobles of the Julio-Claudian period, and so also thereafter. Patricians like Acilius Glabrio, who refused the empire that famous night at the end of the year 192, were certainly not great men, and yet his family boasted descent from Aeneas. We can in fact say just the opposite: late-Roman civilization is rich in very great and indeed gigantic personalities, from Septimius Severus to Diocletian, Constantine and Julian the Apostate, from Tertullian and Origen to Ammianus Marcellinus and St. Augustine. And this prejudice about superior races and superior men, which was so popular at the time of Seeck, no longer tells us anything today. Even the contemporaries of Theognis no longer took account of it and thus created the Hellenic democracies. States do not fall because of the elimination of hypothetical descendents of men who were superior; they do not really fall either because of the diminution of the numbers of those who would have to defend them.

9

Slaves without Family

Like other parts of the inquiry, the investigation of the society and the economic 'style' of the late empire goes back to the sixteenth century. It was presented then as a juridical inquiry. The characteristic form of taxation in the late empire had been the *capitatio-iugatio* which took the shape at once of a tax on the *caput* (on each 'head' of a worker attached to estates) and of a land-tax (on each *iugum* of land). The scholars of the sixteenth and seventeenth centuries asked themselves whether the element of taxation by head predominated in this system or the element of real-property taxation. This was a great question which was widely discussed, with opinion divided between the opposing doctrines of Cujas and Godefroy. The eighteenth century, with its mercantilist outlook, expressed the economic problem of Roman decadence principally in terms of one element, the 'lack of precious metal'. The classic statement of this attitude is by Montesquieu.

'It is known that the mines of Britain were not yet exploited, and that there were very few in Italy and the Gallic provinces, that the mines of Spain were no longer worked from the time of the Carthaginians, or at least were no longer so rich. Thus gold and silver became scarce in Europe; but the emperors wished to impose the same taxation, which ruined everything.'

In our time too some talented scholars, like the German Delbrück and the Englishman Davies, have explained the decadence of the Roman empire by the decline in mineral resources, especially in the west. But this hypothesis is, at the least, insufficient and André Piganiol has rightly insisted on the activity of precious metal mines in Sardinia, Spain and Thrace. On the other hand prospectors for gold in the late empire were subject to heavy taxation and thus to wretched conditions of life which, in the fatal year 378, led them to make common cause with the barbarians in the regions which were occupied. The crisis of the empire was expressed not in the lack of gold and silver but in the tremendous taxation and the monstrous burden which was crushing the workers. Just for this reason the nineteenth century, the century which felt in a special way the problem of the relation between capital and labour, was able to make striking advances in the economic interpretation of the end of the ancient world. It was then that Rodbertus discovered the essential point about capitation; he grasped that this tax showed in a sense that the late empire established a connection between the unit of labour and the unit of land.

The whole labour of research of this great century converged in the work of Max Weber. We all acknowledge, in this exceptionally great historian and sociologist, one of the masters of the contemporary world. He was a free spirit, or rather a liberal, alive to social problems, and is remembered for his political work at the time of the Weimar republic. Long before this, however, as a young man in 1891, he had written a genuine historical masterpiece, *Roman Agrarian History*. He took up some suggestions of Mommsen but followed also his own ideas, in which he could be compared with two Marxists, the German Hartmann and the Italian Ciccotti.

In 1896 he wrote a study of *The Social Origins of the Decline of Ancient Civilisation*. To re-read it after sixty-two years is to marvel; it could have been written yesterday. It was the time when Seeck had just expounded his idea of the 'elimination of the best men'. Max Weber, who did not approve of Seeck's theories, based his essay on the great theme which excited men in the second half of the nineteenth century: the concentration of landed property and the establishment of wage labour.

'The sources give us the clearest picture of the agricultural undertakings of the late republican and early imperial periods. The great landed estate is the essential form of wealth. On the basis of this are raised even the fortunes which are employed in speculation. . . . The management of land is of the plantation type and the workers on the estates are slaves. The *familia* of the slaves and the *coloni*, side by side with each other, are, still in the imperial period, the normal inhabitants of the great estates.

'Let us first of all consider the slaves. What is their condition?

'Let us look at the ideal scheme which has been transmitted to us by the ancient authors of works on agriculture. The dwelling place of the "talking stock" (*instrumentum vocale*), that is the slaves, is to be found near to that of the animals (*instrumentum semivocale*). It consists of the dormitories, the hospital (*valetudinarium*), the prison (*carcer*), the workshop for the workers (*ergastulum*); in short we immediately build up the picture of a barracks. . . . And in fact the slave's life is normally barrack life. They sleep and eat together under the surveillance of the *vilicus*. . . . Work is disciplined in a strictly military fashion. . . . This was indeed essential for, without using the whip, one could not get productive labour from unfree men. But for us one element which can be deduced from this form of barrack life is especially important–the slave living in a barracks not only had no property, he had no family either. Only the *vilicus* lives securely in his separate cell together with a woman in slave marriage (*contubernium*), more or less like the non-commissioned officer in a modern barracks; indeed, according to the writers on agriculture, this arrangement for the *vilicus* is an obligatory rule in the interest of the owners. And, since property and family life are always inter-connected, this relationship can be established also in the case of the *vilicus*; he has his own *peculium*. . . . But the great mass of slaves lack a *peculium* as well as a normal relationship of monogamous union. . . . The absence of the monogamous family leads to other consequences. Man can flourish only in the bosom of the family. Thus the slave barracks, deprived of slave families, cannot reproduce itself independently. To grow and to be renewed it must have recourse to the continual acquisition of slaves. . . . The old slave system consumes men as the blast-furnace consumes coal. The slave market, with a continual new acquisition of human material, is an essential premise for the slave barracks . . . therefore it depends on the uninterrupted importation of men into the market. . . .

'Later writers on agriculture give the impression that the rising price of the human material had led at first to the improvement of technique by means of the development of specialized workers. But after the end of the last wars of aggression in the second century, which had already effectively acquired the character of slave hunts, came the crisis of the great plantations with their slaves to whom marriage and property were denied.

'We can tell that this happened, and how it happened, by comparing the condition of the slaves of the big agricultural undertakings, as they are described by Roman authors, with their condition on the estates of the Carolingian period as we know them from Charlemagne's instructions for his demesnes in the *capitulare de villis imperialibus* and from the monastic surveys of that time. In both these periods we find slaves as agricultural workers, lacking rights and in particular subjected to the absolute authority of the owners of their labour. In these respects then there is no difference. . . . But in another respect there is a difference and a radical one: Roman slaves live communally in slave barracks; the *servus* of the Carolingian period on the other hand lives in a *mansus servilis* on the land which the lord has granted him with the obligation of personal services. Thus the slave is restored to family life and with the family comes also the possession of goods on the part of the slave. This separation of the slave from the *oikos* took place in the late-Roman period and it was in fact bound to be a consequence of the failure of growth in the slave barracks. . . .

'While the slave thus climbed socially up to the position of a peasant obliged to perform personal services, at the same time the *colonus* sank to the position of a peasant bound to the land. . . .

'[On the other hand it was impossible to produce for the market with the simple means offered by the forced labour or personal services of the *colonus*; production organized for sale required the disciplined barracks of slaves.] . . . The chief purpose of the *oikos* is more and more to cover the needs of the landowner through the division of labour. The big estates detach themselves from the city market. . . .

'In the late-Roman period this decadence of the city is affected and determined by the financial policy of the state. This too, with growing financial demands, increasingly takes on the form of natural economy and the treasury becomes an *oikos* which resorts for its needs to the market as little as possible and to its own means as much as possible, in this way *making difficult* the creation of fortunes in money. . . . Indeed with the decadence of the cities and of communications and the collapse into a natural economy the possibility of taxation on a monetary basis became, as far as the countryside was concerned, more and more remote.

'Where therefore, half a millennium later, Charlemagne, that late executor of the will of Diocletian, gave renewed life to the political unity of the west, this process was carried out on the basis of a strictly natural economy. . . .

'The city has disappeared: the Carolingian age knows nothing of the city as a specifically administrative concept. The pillars of civilization are the landed nobility. . . . Civilization has become rural. . . .

'The separate family and private property were given back to the masses of unfree men. They were gradually raised from the status of *instrumentum vocale* into the circle of humanity and their family life was protected with moral guarantees thanks to Christianity. . . . The spiritual life of the west fell into a dark night but its decline recalls that giant of Greek myth who acquired new strength when he rested on the bosom of Mother Earth.'

This long quotation was necessary because Max Weber's essay is really the most fundamental work and the greatest work of genius which has ever been written on the economic crisis of antiquity. It is true that it labours under the severe handicap of the completely adverse judgment of Michael Rostovtzeff. But what matters in Weber's work is the vision of the transition from the monetary economy of the Roman empire to the self-sufficient economy of the Middle Ages through the ruin of the ancient world and of the institutions which had made possible the great supranational unity of Rome. Everything that has been written since Weber about the economic development of the ancient world is connected directly, or quite often indirectly, with his vision. It was already present in the *Roman Agrarian History* of 1891 and it was formulated with superb brilliance in the essay we have been recalling. Later on he developed the same concept in the great 'social and economic history of antiquity' which he published in 1909 under the title *Agricultural relationships in Antiquity* in the *Handwörterbuch der Staatswissenschaften.*

The logical train of his reasoning is clear. City life and the related monetary economy based on commercial transactions were possible only as long as the landed estates were cultivated by slaves in barracks without wives or children. After the end of the wars of conquest and of the importation of slaves which they facilitated, it was necessary to resort to the settlement of slaves with their wives and children or to free *coloni* bound to the estate. But when the slave had a family, the rural economy of the *oikos*–that is to say a closed economy–was substituted for the monetary economy; trading connections disappeared and the treasury, becoming an *oikos* itself, required taxation basically in kind. There are two essential points in this Weberian interpretation. Firstly: the commercial economy was possible only as long as there were barracks of slaves without families and also wars of conquest which guaranteed a continual supply of them. Secondly: the treasury is an *oikos* which could tend towards forms of natural rather than monetary economy. Let us examine these two points, beginning with the first.

Is it true that, as Weber thinks, the economy depending on slaves, lodged in barracks without women or children, declines because of the drying up of the wars of conquest; and that the crisis of this economy, enforcing the grant to the slaves of a woman and a *peculium*, led to the stagnation of trade and therefore to a domestic economy? It is only possible to reply to this after we have considered more closely the important and painful spectacle of the life of the country slave in the Roman world. (City slaves were rather more fortunate in that manumission was much easier for them and their owners were much more closely bound to them.) Let us attempt to investigate the mind of a country slave in the age of Cato and Varro in the second and first centuries B.C., the great age of the slave economy.

By a principle which always reigns unquestioned, this slave, like all men of servile condition, has no rights. Therefore he has no right to love. He really is a talking animal, *instrumentum vocale.* Cato grants him, on certain conditions, occasional and sorry loves, but never true love and still less a permanent partner. Only to the slave who is in charge of the work, the *vilicus* or steward, does Cato allow a female partner, the *vilica*. As far as this goes then Max Weber is undoubtedly right: the slave has no family. But, if we question more deeply the mind of the slave of this age, we begin to sense that he feels the weight of his bestial state of life. He reacts. Cato's little work gives us the picture of rural slavery in the first half of the second century B.C. In the second half of this same century (more precisely in 135–32 and 104–1) there were two great slave rebellions in Sicily. Slaves, men who may not love, see their work as a curse worse than death.[1] They may not love; nor may they drink wine. They are allowed only the *lora*, the drink made from the remains of the pressed grapes which is not alcoholic and is provided as a substitute since it cannot excite them to protest.

But no rational brutalization can destroy the humanity in man. The mind of the slave has not lost that moral consciousness of which men try to deprive him by right of conquest. For example the rebels of 135 B.C. spared the generous daughter of a very cruel slave-owner. Their resentment, however, is as hard as the metal of which the chains are made which when they are recaptured they will carry back to the labour prison.

In these conditions the labour of slaves in a plantation economy cannot be as productive as one might imagine. The Roman slave-owners began to realize the important fact that the slave who is settled on the land, with wife and children, becomes fond of the land and produces more. They did not of course accept all the consequences of this immediately. But there is no doubt that the more intelligent among them made this observation. Varro, who compiled his work on agriculture in 36 B.C. found it already in one of his predecessors, Cassius,[2] who had published his work in 88 B.C. And

[1] Cf. now Vogt, 'Struktur der antiken Sklavenkriege', *Abhandlungen Mainz, Geist. und Soz. Kl.* (1957), p. 1; Burian, *Listy filologické* (1957), pp. 197 ff.

[2] Varro found in Cassius the information that the slaves of Epirus were famous for their attachment to women and children. On the other hand it is known that in 167 B.C. quite 150,000 men of Epirus were taken into slavery 'in a single day' (cf., e.g., Rostovtzeff, *The Social and Economic History of the Hellenistic World* (1941), II, p. 739). I believe that many of these 150,000 slaves on Roman estates were not entirely torn away from their close relations and that, briefly, there were many, many thousands of Epirote slaves on the estates with their wives and children. Thus it seems to me it can be established that the Epirote slave settled apart was more profitable than the slave who was deprived of love and descendants. Knowledge of this fact reached Cassius, whose 'translation' from Mago was really a work rich in ideas quite separate from those of Mago.

we find, even in Cassius, the observation that it is necessary to employ, beside the slaves, free wage-labourers. Even at that time apparently free labour seemed useful in competition with servile labour.

The slave barracks was thus destined to decline because a number of considerations suggested the need to give the slave an interest in production and to give him a family and a plot. In this sense, then, we can partially amend the first point in Weber's theory.[1] It was not the end of the wars of conquest, so much as the simple need for a greater economic output, which often suggested the substitution of the slave settled on land for the slave in barracks and the greater and greater use of another labour force or, as they say, of *coloni*. The plantation economy with slave barracks was at bottom a phenomenon due to the influence of the Carthaginian agricultural system on the Roman. In the Maghreb ruled by Carthage it had been possible for a long time; in the Roman world it was widely undermined by the slave wars of the second and first centuries B.C. and by the subsequent cultural and economic needs. One might perhaps say that this plantation economy was in a sense a parenthesis–though one of great importance–in the history of Italy. Etruria[2] for example had been a classic land of *servi-coloni* with families, the *etera* and *lautni-etera*, and continued to be so even in the second and first centuries when labour from the Hellenistic countries was imported into it. The system of cultivation by slaves settled on the land or free *coloni* might be regarded, in this sense, as the victory of an Italic, or at least Etruscan, tradition over the methods of the great estates of Carthaginian Africa. At any rate the crisis of this system, far from bringing about a halt in the commercial economy, coincided with a revival of economic consciousness inspired by the *nouveau riche* middle class, the Trimalchios of the first century. They seem to have thought that the raising up of the slaves was in the long run an expense worth facing for the sake of having a labour force with a stake in the work and not too hostile. These Trimalchios of the first century A.D. were quite intelligent people. They

[1] Cf. also Westermann in Pauly-Wissowa, *Real-Encyclopädie der classischen Altertumswissenschaft*, Supplement-band VI, pp. 944 ff.; and in general for the Hellenistic age Biezunska-Mallowist, *Eos*, suppl. 20 (1949).

[2] *Historia*, 1957, pp. 110 ff.; cf. ch. 1 above; and in general Bilinski, *Archeologia*, III (1949), pp. 93 ff.

came from the ranks and they could do their sums. Petronius has drawn an unforgettable portrait of one of them for us.

'But a clerk quite interrupted his [Trimalchio's] passion for the dance by reading as though from the gazette: "July the 26th. Thirty [slave] boys and forty [slave] girls were born on Trimalchio's estate at Cumae. Five hundred thousand pecks of wheat were taken up from the threshing-floor into the barn. Five hundred oxen were broken in. On the same date: the slave Mithridates was led to crucifixion for having damned the soul of our lord Gaius [Caligula]. On the same date: ten million sesterces which could not be invested were returned to the reserve. On the same day: there was a fire in our gardens at Pompeii, which broke out in the house of Nosta the bailiff." "Stop," said Trimalchio, "when did I buy any gardens at Pompeii?" "Last year," said the clerk, "so that they are not entered in your accounts yet." Trimalchio glowed with passion, and said, "I will not have any property which is bought in my name entered in my accounts unless I hear of it within six months." We now had a further recitation of police notices, and some foresters' wills . . . then the names of bailiffs. . . .'[1]

The 'Gazette' of Trimalchio's estate is amusing but it is also suggestive. The world of Petronius's story is in fact made up of estates and of slaves who live on them, grow up, and even maybe make their fortune there. In the next century, at the time of Marcus Aurelius and Commodus, Apuleius's novel shows us estates not cultivated by slaves but, on the contrary, by *coloni*. Now servile and free labour are living side by side and approximating increasingly to each other. The principle that it is inhuman to separate the slave from his female partner is being asserted and, on the other hand, the free *colonus* who, as a free man, can never be restricted in his right to have a family, and may smile upon his wife and children after his work is done, has nonetheless to perform labour services to the master. Servile labour had the advantage for the owner that the slaves could never be recruited for military service and this was a significant point which seems to us to have been an important reason for the persistence of slavery. But free labour also had its advantages. In the end there was an equalization of the two types. This change was not determined by the end of the wars of conquest.

[1] Loeb translation.

From the time of Marcus Aurelius and throughout the late empire many defeated barbarians became *laeti*. Thus they were not reduced to slavery but were settled in the countryside to work the lands which were called *laeticae*, and settled of course *cum opibus liberisque*, 'with means of livelihood and children'. Yet, even in the final sunset of Roman greatness under Stilicho, the great victory over Radagaisus resulted in an enormous unloading of Ostrogothic slaves onto the market. In cases like this, the result of victorious war was still the enslavement of the barbarians and not their settlement as *laeti*. But the empire's economic problem was not solved by the introduction of a free barbarian labour force, and still less by the enslavement of defeated barbarians. It had passed beyond the stage where the choice between free and servile labour was decisive.

If we want to examine further the Weberian problem of the relationship between wars of conquest and a slave economy, it will be useful to look at one region of great historical importance: Pannonia. Pannonia, and the whole region of Augustan Illyricum, with Dalmatia, Moesia and Pannonia, included such flourishing cities, on the Danube or not far from it, as Vindobuna, Solva, Aquincum, Carnuntum, Intercisa, Mursa, Cibale, Singidunum and Sirmium, and behind these Sabaena, Poetovio and others. It was a region of great value. Several present-day capitals are within the territories of the cities which have just been listed; Vindobuna is Vienna, Aqincum is Budapest, Singidunum is Belgrade. How then were the lands of this flourishing territory farmed? The great Russian historian, Rostovtzeff, decided, with shrewd intuition, that the Pannonian fields had been cultivated by slaves. Later, Westermann[1] denied that Rostovtzeff's theory was acceptable because, he pointed out, there was no evidence for it in our sources. Who is right; Rostovtzeff or Westermann? As far as the late empire is concerned we can find the answer in a significant text called the *Expositio totius mundi*, an extremely intelligent and detailed geo-economic picture of the Roman world which was compiled at that time. The *Expositio* tells us in detail the products, the economic character and the extent of trade in each region of the empire. Of Pannonia it says, 'Now comes

[1] Westermann, *op. cit.*, p. 1024.

the region of Pannonia, a land rich in everything, especially in fruit, mules, trades and, in part, slaves.' The mention of slaves stands out, for in the whole of its treatment of the economic geography of the Roman world, the *Expositio* mentions the abundance of slaves only in Pannonia (though it is indeed said to be only partial) and Mauretania. And it must be realized of course that Pannonia in Europe and Mauretania in Africa were frontier regions where warlike operations or commercial activity must have contributed notably to the market in slaves even in the late empire.

The consequences of this slave economy were however once again ruinous. The presence of a powerful servile labour force tended to depress free labour and ended by extinguishing the difference in incomes between the theoretically free *colonus* and the peasant-slave with a sturdy barbarian ancestry. The *coloni* of Pannonia continually wanted in fact to flee from the estates, so that the emperors were compelled in 371 to insist on the obligation to serfdom of the *coloni* of this province. Thus Pannonia in the late empire witnessed again the phenomenon which had appeared in Italy and Sicily five centuries earlier, the weariness and impatience of the slaves, with the very serious additional discontent of the *coloni* who were becoming, rather more than in other regions, assimilated to the slaves.

The crisis of the empire was not then due to the drying up of the import of slaves. If anything it was more acute in those very regions where there was a marked presence of slave labour. The Pannonian peasantry were men seized by desperation. They could not pay their taxes. They appealed to the presence of the barbarians as to a liberation. In 406, that crucial moment in the age of Stilicho, they moved from Pannonia towards distant Gaul to take part in the conquest of the empire with the invading barbarians. They were victorious; joined with the barbarians they devastated the west. St. Jerome protests in one of his letters:

'innumerable and ferocious peoples have occupied all the Gauls. All that land which extends from the Alps to the Pyrenees and is bounded by the Ocean and Rhine has been devastated by the Quadi, the Vandals, Sarmatians, Alans, Gepids, Heruli, Saxons and Burgundians, and, o our poor state, the Pannonians too are our enemies.'

This rebellion of the Pannonians[1] is a rebellion of the oppressed who have chosen the way pointed out by desperation. Still earlier than this, in the age of Stilicho, a great rebellion against Rome had started out in 397 from Mauretania, the other region which the *Expositio* selects as rich in slaves and an exporter of this human merchandise. ('Mauretania', says the *Expositio*, 'exports clothes and slaves and abounds in corn.') Though it was subdued by Stilicho, this revolt, in which the 'barbarian' Moorish tribes were led by the Gildo, is extremely significant.

We can now say definitely that the end of the ancient world was not determined by the abandonment of wars of conquest with their trails of wretches dragged into slavery. In short, on this matter, we have parted company with Weber. But the central intuition of Weber's work remains alive: the countryside had increasing importance.[2] The economy became more and more an *oikos* economy[3] and the development of the seigneurial estate divided the city from the countryside. Not that the cities simply declined; on the contrary the great cities of the late empire found their economic power increased, while in many regions, especially the west, the smaller ones languished. Another partial correction that has to be made to Weber's vision is that the commerce of the late empire did not necessarily stagnate. The passages which we have just quoted from the *Expositio totius mundi* about Pannonia and Mauretania are enough to prove the liveliness of their export trades. But there is no doubt that the estate of the late empire, cultivated in part by *coloni* and in part by slaves, tended to become a closed unit.[4] An estate-

[1] The 'revolution' of the Pannonians is thus to be added to the other cases of 'revolution' pointed out by Maschkin, *Römische Geschichte* (German translation, 1953), pp. 632 ff. It is understood of course that in the application of the concept of 'revolution' to the end of the ancient world, one assumes also the presence of the characteristics of a society profoundly different from the modern world. Cf. the methodological limitations formulated by Kovaliov, *Vestnik Drevnej Istorii* (1954), pp. 3, 40 ff.; and by Vittinghoff, *Geschichte in Wissenschaft und Unterricht* (1958), pp. 464 ff.

[2] Cf. recent remarks on the reflection of the phenomenon in ecclesiastical organization by Kirsten, *Reallexikon für Antike und Christentum*, III, p. 1112.

[3] The case of Africa is typical: Piganiol, *Hommage à Lucien Febvre* (1953), I, pp. 67 ff. In general see Courtois, Leschi, Perrat, Saumagne, *Tablettes Albertini*, (1952).

[4] Cf. in general Pallasse, *Orient et Occident à propos du Colonat Romain au Bas-Empire* (1950); *Revue Historique de Droit Français et Etranger* (1958), pp. 67 ff.; Lot, *Nouvelles recherches sur l'impôt foncier et la capitation personelle sous le Bas-Empire* (1955); the discussion in *Vestnik Drevnej Istorii* (1953, 1954, 1955, 1956) between Shtaerman, Kazdan, Korsunski, Kovalev, Siuziumov, Udaltsova, Lipchitz; finally

owner of the late empire writes: 'The presence of the master is the wealth of the estate. . . . It must necessarily contain workers in iron, wood, pottery, so that the lure of the city does not take agricultural labour away from the countryside.' The seigneurial estate of this period is thus an *oikos*, a unit in itself with tendencies towards a natural economy. Is the treasury, that is essentially the Roman state, also an *oikos*? This assertion is what we called the second point in Max Weber's teaching. It is connected with the internal dialectic of the economic process which lies between antiquity and the medieval world,[1] the transition from a monetary economy to a predominantly natural economy. It is one of the antitheses which present themselves to the student of this age of contrast, which are profound yet not always clear. We shall examine it in the next chapter within the framework of the antitheses which dominated the men of that time and still fascinate us in spite of their remoteness.

Shtaerman, *Krizis Rabovladel'ceskovo Stroja v Zapad'nich Provintzijach Rimskoj Imp.* (1957); cf. Djakov, *Vestnik Drevnej Istorii* (1958), pp. 122 ff.

[1] Latouche, *The Birth of Western Economy* (1961).

10

The Economic Problem: Country and City

Max Weber's essay on *The Social Causes of the Decline of Ancient Civilisation* came out in 1896. The questions which it raised still confront every student of the subject with new problems and the great social changes which we have witnessed in this century make us even more acutely interested in Weber's antitheses. What was the relation between natural economy and money economy at the end of the Roman empire? Weber had asserted that even the treasury was an economic unit in itself, an *oikos*. This idea, which Weber himself had formulated very cautiously, was developed with unexpected results by a remarkable young Finnish scholar, Gunnar Mickwitz.

In 1932 Mickwitz published his fundamental work, *Money and Economy in the Roman Empire of the Fourth Century*. Here, for the first time, the problem raised by Weber was related to the other problem of the relationship between the bureaucracy and the tax-payers. Mickwitz, who could perhaps be defined as an extreme Weberian, spoke of a class struggle between the state bureaucracy which wanted payment in kind ('the treasury is an *oikos*') and tax-payers who were trying to pay in money (*adaerare* as it was called) the taxes which the state asked to have as services in kind. One cause of the fall of the ancient world was to be sought in this struggle between natural economy, preferred by the treasury, and money economy, preferred by the taxpayers.

But even this possible 'cause' of the death of Rome appears insufficient for the interpretation of that great phenomenon on the economic plane. On the contrary, one can be sure that in many cases the taxpayers preferred to pay in kind rather than money. '*Adaeratio* offered' (in the fourth and fifth centuries) 'a dangerous margin for abuses of power. Some emperors took notice of this danger; others did not. It depended on the authority which they could exert over a bureaucracy whose abuses were in large measure responsible for the catastrophe.'[1]

Thus the problem broadens out. It becomes once again the whole question of the catastrophe of the Roman Empire in its relation with monetary and economic phenomena in general. To understand it we have to go much further back, as far as the age of Commodus (180–92) when the economic crisis first manifested itself clearly. We may get some suggestions from the history of a bank of the time of Commodus which was managed by the slave-banker Callistus, the man who later, under Elagabalus, became Pope and enriched the history of imperial Rome with his genius and his boundless faith.

The bank directed by Callistus while he was still a slave belonged to his master Carpophorus, an imperial freedman and himself also a slave. It was a bank for Christians in an officially pagan Rome. It accepted deposits from Christians, put the money out at interest, lending for example to Jews, and returned the interest as profits to the small Christian savers; in short it was a bank dealing in deposits and loans. At a certain point it went bankrupt. Carpophorus naturally treated Callistus as the scapegoat and threw him into the *pistrinum*, that living hell where slaves turned the millstone and ground the grain. Later on after he had been freed from the *pistrinum* Callistus was condemned for his Christianity. The bankruptcy of Carpophorus and Callistus and the latter's condemnation are to be dated around 184–8. This was the golden age of the very powerful imperial freedmen, and yet Carpophorus, who was one of them, could not prevent the collapse. When Callistus later came to be in charge of his famous catacombs and then finally Pope, he showed himself to be an excellent administrator. Surely his courage as a

[1] Piganiol, *Journal des Savants* (1955), p. 10.

financier would have saved the bank if the economic circumstances had permitted it. In fact the tendency of the economic circumstances of the age of Commodus was towards inflation and, in the Roman world, inflation always produced a great disequilibrium of interest. Those to whom Callistus had lent substantial sums could no longer pay the high interest rates which were necessary to sustain a bank which was designed largely for charitable purposes. The shipwreck of the bank under Commodus is then symptomatic of a general malaise. The state itself had to steer a difficult course through the dangers of the new economic circumstances. From 184 onwards the Italian property owners could no longer keep up with the interest rates needed by charitable institutions.

What was the origin of this crisis? The question has been much debated in recent times, and one might say that there are two theories about this economic change, which marks the beginning of the late-Roman period. The first theory, originally formulated by Heichelheim and then accepted by Mickwitz and Piganiol, maintains that there was a remarkable price-rise under Commodus, amounting to a price revolution. The other theory, which is supported by Schehl and Passerini,[1] denies altogether that there was a price revolution under Commodus and shifts the crisis to the next epoch, the age of the Severi. This is not a matter of detail but a question of basic importance: what determined the great economic crisis of the Roman empire? Those who deny the existence of the price revolution under Commodus argue something like this: Commodus was a peaceful emperor who tried to preserve the purity of the silver coinage (the *denarius*); so there was no economic crisis under Commodus. This reasoning does not take account of some extraordinary elements in the late-Roman epoch and especially in the work of that complex and strange son of Marcus. Commodus tried to keep the silver content of the *denarius* intact, avoiding the material expression of inflation which would be given by the reduction of the fineness of the silver in the *denarius*. He tried to keep prices down by price controls.[2] Of course this young Roman Hercules, who loved his

[1] Passerini, 'Sulla pretesa rivoluzione dei prezzi durante il regno di Commodo' in *Studi in onore di Gino Luzzatto* (1949).

[2] In an epigraphic text of Henchir Snobbeur (*C.I.L.*, VIII, 23956; see Merlin, *Ins. latines de la Tunisie*, no. 676) Commodus mentions the price of a slave *ex forma censoria* (500 denarii, not a high price). His maximum price list (whose extent however is

populace so much that he offered them the spectacle of his own imperial gladiatorial skill, did not waver in the assurance that he had found the remedy for a sick economy. But Commodus's good coinage did not in fact stave off inflation.

This paradox is really no paradox. We have to consider the economic facts in the context of the spiritual climate in which they appeared. Monetary phenomena are not enough to determine a crisis. Even if Commodus's *denarius* had retained the same fineness of silver that it had had under his father Marcus, the agony of the old economic system would not have been averted. Only after Commodus is silver money definitely inflated, by Septimius Severus, who brings about a change from an alloy including 25–30 per cent of copper to one with 50 per cent of copper, a radical depreciation of the *denarius*. But the transformation of the currency by Septimius Severus was only a consequence of the crisis, not the crisis itself, which already existed under Commodus as a result of the plagues and the wars of the age of Marcus.

An epidemic is a sickle which reaps pitilessly, scattering death abroad. At Rome under the same Commodus, in certain periods of the year 189, 2,000 men a day died of the plague. If the sickness had not been checked the whole population of the city would have disappeared in one year. In these circumstances measures undertaken by the state, like Commodus's list of maximum prices, were no more than rough palliatives. The urban population of Rome continued to suffer dreadfully. There are no magical remedies to deal with hunger. In hopelessly unfavourable circumstances even good intentions seem to be deceptions. So, when grain was short, the Roman masses rebelled against the imperial freedman Cleander, whom Commodus had appointed praetorian prefect. It was a dangerous moment and Commodus, with the advice of Marcia, had to sacrifice his prefect. In the provinces the crisis struck especially at Gaul, where military conscription continually snatched hands from the fields: hence the desperate revolution of a Gallic peasant who

unknown to us) is attested by the *Historia Augusta*, according to which it had no success because goods disappeared from the market (*vilitatem proposuit, ex qua majorem penuriam effecit*; in the maximum price list of Diocletian the same terms, *vilitas* and *penuria*, recur). On economic planning in general, of which the maximum prices are the characteristic expression, see Piganiol, *Scientia* (1947), pp. 95 ff.; Lambrechts, *Antiquité Classique* (1949), pp. 109 ff., Cf. ch. 6 above.

organized a band of brigands and got as far as conceiving an attempt on Commodus's life. This was a crisis, then, which dripped with the blood and the sufferings of the provincials, not an economic and demographic crisis but also spiritual and political. The more inexorable it appeared the greater became Commodus's obsession with his inability to placate the mob by his Herculean presence in the circus and the amphitheatre, and with the confiscation of the property of condemned senators. On the last night of 192, after a reign of thirteen years, he was overthrown by a conspiracy in which his own companion Marcia took part.

The year of the five emperors was 193, from which emerged the founder of the line of the Severi, Septimius Severus. Septimius devalued the *denarius* and the inflation which this produced seemed to be at last a remedy to the economic crisis. But in fact the distrust of the silver money (the *denarius*) lasted on after him. No one now willingly exchanged the good gold coinage, the *aureus*, which was not easily adulterated, for the devalued silver currency, which was theoretically, according to the emperor, equivalent to one-twenty-fifth of the *aureus* but actually worth scarcely one-fiftieth. Commodus's solution imposed by authority–the maximum prices and the maintenance of the fineness of the silver *denarius*–had proved inadequate. But equally inadequate was the plainly inflationist solution of Septimius Severus. Anyone who wanted to change an *aureus* on the black market would have found someone or other ready to give him more than the 25 *denarii* which was the official exchange rate. Now there was, as always in this age of paradoxical contradictions, a divorce between reality and theory. And between them sprang up the tendency towards a natural economy. Now the man who received his *salarium* in gold (*salarium militiae in auro*) considered himself to be in an impregnable position, secure from deceits and from the contradictions of the theory. The man paid in gold felt himself almost paid in kind, or even better. In the futile list of maximum prices fixed by Commodus a slave cost 500 *denarii* in silver money. Under the Severi it was 2,500. But the man who paid in gold would have found it hard to pay out those 100 *aurei* which were theoretically equivalent to 2,500 *denarii*.

This situation continued, more or less, throughout the third century. In this field too the great revolutionary was Constantine. He created a stable and sound gold coinage, the *solidus*, which was to dominate the whole Byzantine period for centuries and centuries. Therefore the age of Constantine is in a sense the opposite of the third century. In the earlier period the issue of gold coinage was reduced; now on the other hand it was abundant. Then there had been inflation of smaller units of money, now instead they were normally tied to gold.

This explains why in the fourth century *adaeratio* could be attractive to bureaucrats and soldiers. An economy tied to gold was a safeguard against the fluctuations of the market. It was in the fourth century that the rhetorician Libanius recommended to a friend that he should take his remuneration in money and not in kind.[1] Constantine's innovation had had an enormous importance. But it was not appreciated by the masses. They could not pay taxes calculated in gold if they did not possess any gold. Everywhere in the empire the peasant masses felt themselves crushed under the weight of the new economy. The small peasant-proprietors turned themselves into *dediticii* of the rich, or as they were called in Celtic *vassi*: these are the first hints of the economic system of vassalage which marks the Middle Ages. Small men took refuge under the patronage of great landed lordships, which alone could drive away the spectre of the intolerable exactions. In the west it was thought to put an end to all this by reducing the issue of gold money, by, amongst other things, minting smaller gold coins. The name of the new coins, *tremisses*, was on the lips of right-thinking people as a discovery of the good old days–of Alexander Severus, it was said. But every extreme deflationary effort in conditions of insufficient productivity brought the society nearer to a natural economy.

Thus they set off towards the Middle Ages. The huge economic crisis of the late empire, resulting from the lack of balance between productivity and the needs of centralization, led to the decline of the supranational unity based on a money economy. The economic manifestation of the crisis thus shows us what we might almost call its 'mathematical' side: a deflation without corresponding productivity led to the collapse of the economic framework.

The human side of the crisis is however beyond this mathematical

[1] Petit, *Libanius et la vie municipale à Antioche au IVe siècle* (1955), p. 303.

formula. The history of material culture is, before everything, the history of culture: of the *tragédie* and *comédie humaine*.

Beside the antithesis of natural economy and money economy the ancient world also embraced the antithesis between rural masses and city middle class. As far as it concerns the Roman empire this problem is at the heart of another fundamental work, the *Social and Economic History of the Roman Empire* by Michael Rostovtzeff, published in 1926. This historian saw in the crisis of the empire the results of a conflict between peasantry and urban middle classes, which might be considered analogous to that which developed in the early part of the Leninist revolution between the kulaks and the labouring populations of the cities. He had been led to this new interpretation not only by an emotional reflection on this aspect of the Russian revolution but also, on the plane of scholarship, by the consideration that as early as the third century and throughout the late empire the Roman army was recruited from the rural masses. He concluded that this army, composed of peasants, was a natural enemy of the city middle classes. Therefore in his *History*, which covered the period from Augustus to Diocletian, the emphasis was placed on the last part of the second and, especially, on the third century. This conflict between peasant soldiers and city middle class seemed to him to be already manifested in the violence with which the soldiers of Septimius Severus hurled themselves against Byzantium (196) and against Lyons (197). But the centre of these events in his account, the point at which the conflict seems to reach a crisis and reveal itself in its full seriousness, is the year 238, the year of the rebellion against the Emperor Maximinus Thrax. One might say that it is this brutal and powerful soldier who stands out amongst the protagonists of Rostovtzeff's *History*: a man who knew how to defeat the Germans but not how to make himself loved by the senate and who comes down to us under the weight of a senatorial tradition which was relentless in its condemnation of him.

'The events in Africa are generally misrepresented by modern scholars, who persist in speaking of a peasant revolt, in face of the clear statement of Herodian, our best source, who was misunderstood and mistranslated by the Latin biographer of Maximinus. What really happened was as follows. After the accession of Maximinus the procurator of Africa received a commission to extort money there for the emperor. That he was appointed governor of the province in place of the aged proconsul M. Antonius Gordianus. who retired to the city of Thysdrus, is a very attractive hypothesis of von Domaszewski. The procurator, reluctantly helped by the quaestor and his assistants, proceeded in the usual ruthless manner and attacked particularly the rich landowners of the province, who formed, as we know, the most influential portion of the population of the African cities. Some of these men, described by Herodian as "well-born and rich", being threatened with the prospect of losing their "paternal and ancestral estates", organized a plot. To ensure its complete success, they ordered some of the *oiketai* (slaves or tenants, probably the former) to come from their estates to the city armed with axes and sticks. Such a crowd would not look suspicious to the procurator, who was accustomed to receive from the peasants complaints against their landlords. These men killed the procurator, and thereupon the leaders of the plot, a group of African landowners, whose numbers were increased by other men of the same class, proclaimed Gordian emperor. Gordian, however, did not succeed in receiving any support from the African army. His forces were a motley crowd consisting of a few soldiers (perhaps the *cohors urbana* of Carthage) and a militia composed of men who dwelt in the cities, probably the members of the *curiae iuniorum*. They were attracted by Gordian's promise to banish all the spies and to restore the confiscated estates. These troops were badly equipped and badly organized. They had no weapons and used such as were to be found in the houses of the African *bourgeoisie*–swords, axes, and hunting javelins (the equipment of hunters may be seen on numerous African mosaics). It is hardly probable that many peasants and tenants joined his standard. No wonder that his army was easily vanquished by the regular troops of Africa, led by the Numidian *legatus* Capelianus, his personal enemy. The victory was followed by an orgy of murder and confiscation. Capelianus first executed all the aristocracy of Carthage and confiscated both their private fortunes and the money belonging to the city and the temples. He then proceeded to do the same in the other cities, "killing the prominent men, exiling the common citizens, and ordering the soldiers to burn and pillage the estates and the villages."

'Meanwhile Gordian had been recognized at Rome, and the

Romans, even after his death, persisted in their revolt against Maximinus. The revolt spread quickly all over Italy and assumed the same form as the revolt of Africa: it was a desperate fight of the city *bourgeoisie* against the soldiers and their leader, the soldier-emperor.' . . . 'I do not doubt that Maximin was an honest man and an able general. But his aim was to destroy the main fabric of the Roman state, as based on the cities. No wonder that he was hated by those who saw in such destruction the fall of ancient civilization as a whole–which indeed it really was. How could they believe in the necessity of it, if even modern scholars are not all convinced that it was necessary to crush the educated classes in order to bring about an alleged equality that was never achieved?'[1]

This passage by Rostovtzeff on the African movements against Maximinus, which reduces the events to the city-countryside antithesis, is directed against, and at the same time closely connected with, a passage by Otto Seeck. Seeck also had emphasized the importance of that revolt, which appeared to him, preoccupied as he was with studying the 'elimination of the best', as a consequence of the barbarization which he believed to have taken place after the settlement of *laeti* inside the empire from the time of Marcus onward. Seeck's interpretation falls–as far as the cultural 'barbarization' of the peasants is concerned–together with his famous premise, the 'elimination of the best'. But we cannot completely accept Rostovtzeff's theory either. One cannot really see any solidarity between peasants and soldiers against the cultured classes in the events of 238.[2] Herodian, the principle source of information on the revolt, tells us that 'relatives and domestics abused the soldiers, thinking that Maximinus himself was doing these things through their action. . . . Maximinus's legate ordered the soldiers to burn and plunder fields and villages'.

There was in reality no genuine solidarity between peasants and soldiers as far as the revolt of 238 in Africa is concerned. And again in Egypt, under Decius, we hear of some peasants who go from a wedding feast to attack and put to flight 'with a single attack' the

[1] Rostovtzeff, *Social and Economic History of the Roman Empire* (second edition, revised by P. M. Fraser, 1957), I, pp. 455–7, II, p. 734.

[2] Cassola, *Nuova Rivista Storica* (1957).

soldiers who had arrested Bishop Dionysius of Alexandria.[1] The city-country antithesis therefore cannot be converted straightforwardly into a city-soldiery antithesis. As for the complex phenomenon of the 'reawakening of the peasants' in the imperial period, it was never a unified phenomenon, nor always conscious. Being the product of a complex and many-sided disquiet, it cannot easily be reduced to a single description. Furthermore there was, either secretly in their hearts or openly in rebellions, the weariness or simply protest of the peasants against the fiscal oppression. But there was also the protest of the rural masses about the wages denied by their masters or unpaid (one should not forget the epistle of St. James as early as the first century of the empire); and sometimes on the imperial estates there is the unhappiness of peasants oppressed by extortionate administrators. . . . These protests and this weariness called forth a kind of national consciousness in some areas, the chivalrous pride of the Celtic peasant and the powerful personality of the Syrian *colonus* begin to act. We can circumscribe the conflict between peasants and upper classes within these limits. Behind the multitudes of peasants appears the first timid manifestation of the 'nations', the *ethne*, which according to the biblical exegesis of St. Hippolytus, would destroy the Roman empire at the end of the world.

[1] Eusebius, *H.E.*, VI, 40, 5–9. (Note that it is not a matter of peasants who are declared Christians: in fact the bishop, even when he has grasped their friendly intentions, begs them to cut his head off.)

11

Nations, 'Democracies', Liberty

'Liberty and the nations' is in a sense a new theme as far as the history of the Roman empire is concerned.[1] It can however be connected with the problems raised by Rostovtzeff and also with the theme of the dissatisfaction of the peasant masses forced to live within the composite unity of the great empire. In this field as in others the new features which are most significant for the crisis of the ancient world appear in the age of Commodus (180–92) and the Severi (193–235).

Was it possible to bring the masses closer to the Hellenistic-Roman culture of the upper classes? The wars of Marcus Aurelius had deepened the weariness of the provincials under the burden of tributes. At that time a Christian oracular poet sees in the end of the empire the liberation of each *ethnos* from the Roman 'yoke'.[2] *Ethnos* suggests 'nation', a concept which was always connected in the Roman world more or less with language,[3] but never reached as far as the clear idea of the nation-state and appeared rather as a peripheral concept, in contrast with the city-state and the supranational state. While the Christian poet under Marcus Aurelius was

[1] E. L. Woodward's *Christianity and Nationalism in the Later Roman Empire* (1916), should however be mentioned.

[2] *Or. Sib.*, VIII, 126–7.

[3] This is clear from the Achaemenid inscriptions, where the peoples subject to the Persians are listed in the text as 'tongues' (*lisani*).

dreaming of the liberation of every *ethnos* at the end of the empire, which he thought was near at hand, the official Roman state under the same emperor was, on the other hand, praying to its gods for the safety of the subject 'nations'. The priestly college of the *Fratres Arvales* in their annual prayers addressed to Jupiter Optimus Maximus their petition for the safety of 'the Roman Empire, the army, associates, the *nationes* which are *sub dicione* of the Roman people of the *Quirites*'. Marcus Aurelius's son, Commodus, put an end to his father's wars; he hoped that the *nationes* would feel relief and that the peasants of the provinces would welcome the peace joyfully.

We asked earlier whether it was possible to divest these masses of their 'national' characteristics of language and custom? To put it more precisely, was it possible to bring them into still closer relation to the state, by assimilating their traditions and cults to those of the classical Greco-Roman inheritance? This was the great ambition of Caracalla. Giving citizenship to all the free inhabitants of the provinces (except the *dediticii*) in 212 he declared that he wanted on the religious plane to unify the cults of the provincials and of the state. Indeed, in an inscription recently discovered at Dmeir[1] in Syria he makes a show of favour to a certain Aur. Carzaeus, one of the provincials to whom he had newly given citizenship, at the expense of an old Roman citizen; and his sympathy for Aur. Carzaeus is in particular an act of respect for the devotion of the peasantry of the place for their Zeus Hypsistos. In reality, Caracalla's new citizens express the old spirit of the provinces where romanization finds it hard to penetrate the lower classes. Caracalla hopes to overcome 'national' barriers by drawing to himself favoured individuals from the agrarian masses. He knew that these 'national' barriers operated within the empire to its disadvantage.

At the time of Caracalla (or of the Severi in general) the philosophical idea of liberty was put in relation to the idea of the 'nation' for the first time by a great thinker, Bardesanes, a Christian of Edessa. Edessa was the capital of the state of Osrhoene, whose king, Abgar IX, had been converted to Christianity and persecuted the

[1] Roussel-De Visscher, *Syria* (1942–3), pp. 173 ff.; cf. Arangio Ruiz, *B.I.D.R.* (1948), pp. 46 ff.; Kunkel, *Festschrift Lewald*, pp. 81 ff.; Wenger, *Mélanges Grégoire*, III, pp. 469 ff.

worshippers of the goddess Atargatis. In 213 Caracalla deposed Abgar IX and incorporated Osrhoene into the Roman empire. Bardesanes was a fairly influential man at the court of Abgar IX, master of the great Syriac 'national' literature which was destined to have great importance in the eastern part of the Roman empire. In working out a connection between the idea of liberty and that of the nations ('countries'), he was not concerned with liberty in its strictly political sense, which had been an object of inquiry for the men of the Greek democracies. He was concerned more with the problem of liberty as a spiritual fact, briefly as human free will independent of the influence of the planets and the Zodiac. He held that freedom of this kind revealed itself in the national characteristics of the different peoples. His *Dialogue on the Laws of the Countries* has come down to us. It is to be identified with, or at least is connected with, a book of his *On Destiny*, dedicated to a certain *Antoninus* who is in all probability Caracalla himself.[1] In this *Dialogue* Bardesanes's view ranges widely over the world. Everywhere the different nations have differing customs and laws, and in this is revealed human freedom, independent of the horoscope.

'Men have indeed established laws in each country according to that freedom which was given to them by God. In fact the gift of liberty is opposed to the Fate of the Powers, so that they do not assume that which was not given to them. I shall relate, as far as I recall, starting from the East which is the beginning of the whole world.'

Thus Bardesanes speaks of the various customs of the peoples, from the humane Chinese, whose 'freedom Ares does not restrict in such a way that they should scatter the blood of a companion with the sword', to the Indians, Persians, Geti, Kushanites, Recamites, Edessenes, and Arabs, to the Germans, Celts and Britons and so forth. 'Fate cannot compel the Chinese to commit murders, because they do not will it, nor the Brahmans to eat meat, nor the Persians

[1] It is generally thought to be Elagabalus. But at c. 607 Edessa would seem to be still independent. In contrast to the 'Arabs' of c. 603 whose religious customs are changed by the supervening Roman conquest, at Edessa the customs established by Abgar IX continue and no more worshippers of Atargatis are found there. The *Dialogue* seems to me therefore to be earlier than 213. On Bardesanes cf. e.g. Levi Della Vida, *Rivista Trimestrale di Studi Filosofici e Religiosi* (1920), pp. 399 ff.; Schaeder, *Zeitschrift für Kirchengeschichte* (1932), pp. 21 ff.; Cerfaux, *Reallexikon für Antike und Christentum*, pp. 1176 ff.

to avoid marriage with daughters and sisters . . . nor the Britons to avoid polyandry, nor the Edessenes to depart from chastity, nor the Greeks to cease from nude gymnastics, nor the Romans not to conquer territories. . . .' Thus in a work addressed to a member of the imperial Roman family (the 'Antoninus' who may, as we suggested, be Caracalla) Bardesanes placed the Romans on the same level as the other people, barbarian and civilized all together. Their 'national' custom of annexing territories seemed to him on the same plane as, for example, the national custom of polyandry amongst the Britons, or incest amongst Persians or the palestra amongst the Greeks. Thus the Roman idea of supranationalism was reduced to an ordinary custom, no matter whether good or bad, like all the others. The diverse laws of countries govern the philosophical intelligence of this great Syrian and in the varying nature of peoples he sees the freedom of the will revealed. It would be difficult to find another work in which the individuality of the nations is emphasized with such interest, and it is worth underlining once again that Bardesanes wrote at the time of the Severi, the dynasty which attempted consistently and by various means from 193 to 235 to strengthen imperial unity above national characteristics. In Bardesanes's scheme of things the Romans confirm the doctrine of free will by their capacity for changing the laws of countries by armed conquest: 'yesterday again the Romans have conquered the Arabs and abolished all the previous laws [of that region], . . . : thus one who has free will obeys the law which was imposed by another who also has free will'. But Bardesanes also recognizes a higher freedom, which unites the Christians to each other. This Christian liberty rises above national characteristics: 'in whatever country and place they may find themselves the laws of the countries do not divide them from the law of their Christ.'

Implicitly and almost without realizing it, Bardesanes superimposes the Christian supranationalism on that other supranational idea which had inspired the foundation of the Roman empire. We have no grounds for supposing that he was hostile to the Roman empire and, if anything, we should be entitled to take the opposite view. Nevertheless his new perspective, in which the national characteristics of the peoples have an unexpectedly prominent position, implicitly suggests a comparison between the pure idea of

Christian unity and the supranational government of the Romans, based on that tendency to conquest which he considered to be a characteristic of them.

Another Christian contemporary of Bardesanes really was hostile to the Romans: Hippolytus the dissident bishop of Rome. As we have seen earlier, Hippolytus thought that at the end of the empire, which equalled for him the end of the world, ten democracies would have stripped the Romans of their power, dividing it 'according to nations', *kata ethne*. And he also said, in his writing on *Antichrist*, that the Roman empire 'rules over all against their will' and, in his *Commentary on Daniel*, that the Roman supranational unity was a Satanic counterfeit of Christian unity. The concept of 'nations', which he set over against the 'Satanic' empire of Rome, was certainly not foreign to the climate of thought of his age. Something was corroding deeply the great Roman supranational structure. The most striking symptom of this was the formation of the Syriac and Coptic 'national' literatures, bred almost by the religious demands of the masses. But also in the west Irenaeus, the master of Hippolytus, had preached in Celtic to peasants of Gaul and, just as Syriac was being spoken in the neighbourhood of Antioch about 400, so also Celtic was being spoken at the same time around Trier.[1] The 'national' languages pressed up to the gates of the capitals, as if to draw attention to the fact that unity had not been attained, in that great kaleidoscope in which many peoples could not present a single image. Though the Roman state tried in every way to maintain official ignorance of this re-awakening of nationality,[2] reality was every day belying the official assumptions. When the empire was Christianized, Coptic and Syriac 'nationalities' found their lasting expression in the monasteries of Egypt and Syria. The Egyptian monks persistently opposed the military conscription ordered by the Emperor Valens at the most tragic moment of imperial history

[1] The first point is well known from a frequently cited passage of St. John Chrysostom (cf. Paran, *La Crisi della Scuola nel IV secolo d. C.* (1952), pp. 150–3). The second may be demonstrated from the prologue to the second book of St. Jerome's Commentary on the Epistle of St. Paul to the Galatians (this passage in St. Jerome is also important because it attests that as early as his time the Latin language 'changes every day according to the regions and the time': the forerunner of the Romance vernaculars).

[2] When a *candidatus* of Constantius goes to visit the monk Hilarion Constantius does not arrange for him to be accompanied by any interpreter for the Syriac language. (Migne, *Patrologia Latina*, XXIII, p. 39.)

(375).[1] These monks, whom Georges Sorel perspicaciously likened to the Mafia, were, more simply, the bearers of national cultures rooted in the soil of Egypt and Syria, resistent to the aristocratic imposition of the Greco-Roman culture. In Africa the resistance of the native substratum, which still spoke Punic and Berber, was rather more conspicuous and violent in the age of the Christianized empire. It gave rise to the Donatist movement[2] and to its extreme wing, the *Circumcelliones*.

These 'national' upheavals were certainly not in themselves a unique 'cause' of the death of Rome. Without the external shock of the Germans in the west and the Arabs in the east, they would not have acquired the decisive importance which they actually came to have. But, even apart from the Germanic and Arab attack, the empire found itself disarmed in face of the national ferments. Based as it was on Greco-Roman culture, it could not admit the elevation of Coptic or Syriac, Punic or Celtic to the rank of an official language. The greatest revolutionary of the imperial period, Constantine, dared to Christianize the empire but not to broaden the Greco-Roman cultural substance. That is to say, he accepted the victory of the Christian religious sense, which had already appeared to Tertullian as a revolt 'against the old ways' (*adversus vetustatem*), and he accepted it sincerely, himself believing in the God of the Christians. Still, the revolt 'against the old ways', of which Tertullian had spoken, went beyond the mere acceptance of Christianity. New forces which had been held in check for centuries were pressing from below. Culture was being democratized even in the matter of bureaucratic language. The Roman state no longer spoke officially of the *aureus* but rather the *solidus*, no longer of *legatus ad corrigendum statum* but of *corrector*; in this way the language of common speech was being introduced into official statements. But it was the common Latin speech (or Italian as it was called). The culture of the empire remained basically Greco-Roman, and this remains true even for the Byzantine period.[3] National cultures like the Syriac

[1] On the character of the recruitment ordered by Valens, cf. the recent work of Pallasse, *Revue Historique du Droit Français et Etranger* (1958), p. 70.

[2] Willis, *St Augustine and the Donatist Controversy* (1950); Frend, *The Donatist Church* (1952).

[3] Zilliacus, *Zum Kampf der Weltsprachen im oströmischen Reich* (1935). One must however remember that the two *partes* of the empire, east and west, tended more and

and the Coptic continued to go their own way. The problem of the peasant masses, to which Rostovtzeff usefully drew the attention of historians, appears to us, then, as a problem of subject, but unassimilated, nations. They gave rather more than they received; the new antiquantitative and psalmodic music of the Roman world was a gift of the Judaic genius and of the Syriac masses.

more to be differentiated linguistically. Cf. also Courcelle, *Les Lettres Grecques en Occident* (1948); Bardy, *La Question des Langues dans l'Eglise ancienne* (1938).

12

The Institutional Problem

When Rostovtzeff published his great *History* in 1926 the theme 'the end of the ancient world' was everywhere regarded with a mixture of apprehension and keen human interest. The historians of that generation had seen the collapse with the Great War of state structures which were linked in ideas, even to extent of the title of Kaiser or Czar, with Roman Caesarism. The Romanovs, the Habsburgs and the Hohenzollern had fallen. The fall of the Roman empire of the west, and the whole end of the ancient world in general, seemed like a model of the present time; *de te fabula narratur*. In 1923 a historian from Lund, Axel Persson, had thought to find in the social history of the late empire a series of events comparable with those of the Russian Revolution. His comparison, however, concerned only the social aspect of the problem. The fall of the great Russian, Habsburg and German empires also made acute the institutional problem of the relationship between the idea of liberty and the end of the ancient world.[1] About the same time it inspired some essays, which became famous, by the celebrated Spanish thinker Ortega, by an English historian Heitland, and by the Italian Guglielmo Ferrero. To get an idea of the effect of these writings it is enough to think of Georges Sorel, who as far back as 1901 had published a book with

[1] For the presuppositions of this theme in the culture of Libertinism and the Enlightenment cf. De Caprariis, *Rivista Storica Italiana* (1955), pp. 176 ff.

the title *Ruine du Monde Antique* and now felt drawn to revise it for a second edition in 1922, as a result of the publication of Ferrero's book with the same title. It seemed to him indeed that Ferrero's book, with its statement of the question in institutional terms, was clearly opposed to the materialist conception of history. But the most lively of these books, inspired by the institutional interpretation of the crisis, was certainly Ortega's. According to Ortega, the crisis of the Roman imperial state consisted of the inability to substitute new arrangements of representative democracy for the structure of the old state. This is a point of view[1] open to obvious criticism for we cannot expect the ancient world to exhibit constitutional developments which are characteristic of our own time. It may also be pointed out that the Roman world did have examples of provincial assemblies. The problem is rather more complicated: how to assimilate the peasant masses speaking Coptic, Syriac and so on. This could not have been done simply by means of juridical institutions, for cultural factors have their own irrepressible logic.

Ortega's interpretation is interesting in another way for its very modern side. From Polybius onwards, Roman decline was always seen as the disappearance of something perfect. Take for instance the judgment (1583) of Antonio Agostino, Bishop of Lerida. According to this humanist, 'the Romans lost their liberty and their empire over the provinces when they abandoned their ancient customs and institutions'. For Antonio Agostino the main blame fell on Tribonianus, the interpolator of the Roman laws. Or there is Gibbon, for whom the end of the empire was due to the transformation of 'civil society' after the flourishing times of the Antonines. In short it had always been presupposed, in investigating the end of the ancient world, that the abandonment of ancient institutions was the cause, or at least the symptom, of the great crisis. This prejudice in fact seems completely tautological. Ortega's formulation turns these premises upside down. He is not interested in the comparison with a previous institutional reality which would seem better but, on the contrary, in the inability of the Romans to devise new forms for new problems. Here Ortega is the man of our age par excellence, looking forward towards a possible future which yet never existed. Even for this point of view, the contradictions in his thought are

[1] It may be compared with Heitland's.

interesting. Though he was himself an unreserved classicist, under the influence especially of Renan, and an admirer of traditional Roman liberty (that 'freedom without a king' to which he devoted in 1936 the best pages of his *Historia como sistema*), he did not hesitate to condemn Roman traditionalism as responsible for the end of the ancient world. In spite of his classicism Ortega lived in the world of pure historical possibilities. *Las virtudes que no tenemos son las que más importan.*

His interpretation of historical facts was in essence a basically aristocratic interpretation. He could even be considered as the last disciple of Montesquieu. *La rebelión de las masas* is in part intended as an explanation of the end of the ancient world, seen as the paradigm of the end of an aristocratic civilization. This aspect of it recalls the conclusion of Rostovtzeff's *Social and Economic History*, which we have already mentioned:

'Is it possible to extend a higher civilization to the lower classes without debasing its standard and diluting its quality to the vanishing point? Is not every civilization bound to decay as soon as it begins to penetrate the masses?'

But Rostovtzeff as the great historian had wanted to keep on his guard against abstract statements. Not so Ortega. He had an instinctive revulsion from what he called the 'epochs of Kali'.

'The history of the Roman Empire is also the history of the uprising of the Empire of the Masses, who absorb and annul the directing minorities and put themselves in their place. Then also is produced the phenomenon of agglomeration, of "the full". For that reason, as Spengler has very well observed, it was necessary, just as in our own day, to construct enormous buildings. The epoch of the masses is the epoch of the colossal. The tragic thing about this process is that while these agglomerations were in formation there was beginning that depopulation of the countryside which was to result in an absolute decrease of the number of inhabitants in the Empire.'[1]

These formulations of unconcealed, though only partial, Spenglerian origin may contain strands of truth, but the truth in this case is mixed up with errors which in a sense vitiate the substance. It is true that mass movements are characteristic of imperial history, especially the history of the late empire. But one has to distinguish

[1] From Ortega y Gasset, *The Revolt of the Masses*, Allen and Unwin.

clearly between the masses of the big cities, especially Rome, and the proletarian masses of the provinces. As for the agglomerations, these persist only in the great cities (fourth-century Rome, according to calculations which seem fairly probable, had something like 300,000 inhabitants receiving public distributions).[1] The small cities diminished strikingly in importance, enclosed within their restricted walled enclosures. Furthermore one must be careful to avoid the idea that the masses were simply substituted for the ruling classes. Roman traditionalism acted as a limitation to what might be called the 'democratization of culture' so that the senatorial ruling class was always the essential nucleus which gave leadership to the empire and hindered, in effect, rule by the masses. No doubt the new religion which changed the face of the Roman state had arisen from the complaint of the provincial peasant masses, oppressed by masters and tributes, and this cry had reached the lord god of the armies. But the structure of the Christian empire as it was organized by Constantine was essentially a pyramidal society in which the *potentiores* stood at the top and the peasant masses were (following the early lament of the anonymous writer whom we have placed in the age of Julian) *afflicta paupertas*; afflicted, that is, by the tributes and compelled to take refuge in the protection of the old ruling classes.

Representatives of the lower classes, who eventually penetrated through military service into the ruling class, assimilated themselves unquestioningly, as far as mentality and style of living were concerned, to the ruling class. Men of the municipal middle class, who succeeded in attaining the rank of *clarissimi* (meaning membership of the senatorial class) through the bureaucracy, ended still more readily by assimilating themselves unreservedly to their colleagues. The hierarchies of the Christian Church had been rather more open to the lower classes, at one time for instance able to accept a slave who became pope, and a pope of revolutionary spirit too, St. Callistus. But, as the Christian empire went on, men of the ruling classes more and more filled the high ecclesiastical offices, the most illustrious and remarkable case being that of St. Ambrose who was born into a family of *clarissimi* and was himself governor of Liguria. A

[1] Chastagnol, *Revue Historique* (1953), pp. 13 ff. For Antioch, Petit, *Libanius et la Vie Municipale à Antioche* (cf. Ensslin, *Historia*, 1957, p. 377).

contemporary of Ambrose at Rome was Pope Damasus, who came to the pontifical see as candidate of the Roman aristocracy against the Anti-Pope Ursinus. One of the most persistent spokesmen of the pagan aristocracy of Rome, Vettius Agorius Praetestatus, was famous amongst other things for a remark addressed to Pope Damasus: 'Make me pope and I will become a Christian'. This reconciliation between the ruling classes of the state and the superior ecclesiastical hierarchies became more complete in the fifth century, especially with Pope Leo.

Ortega's formula that the masses of the late empire replaced the ruling class is then rather questionable. And how much more questionable is the other famous but vast generalization which he wanted to apply to the end of Roman civilization: *los demagogos han sido los grandes estranguladores de civilizaciones.* The fact is that Roman civilization of the imperial period knew no demagogues, unless one means by this word the great Christian martyrs who gave the masses the new slogan *adversus vetustatem.* The late republic on the other hand certainly had demagogues when it was moving towards the constitutional form of the empire–the name of one of them was Julius Caesar.

In the last analysis the aristocratic interpretation of history fails just at the problem which appears most central to it, the problem of the 'democratization of culture', because it contains contradictions. On the one hand Ortega would have an empire which created a representative democracy, but on the other hand he bewails the non-existent replacement of the ruling class by the masses. The critical relationship in the great civilizations is that between the ruling classes and the masses but this is not–it is worth repeating–a matter of constant or abstract relationship. Nevertheless, in spite of this fundamental mistake, which is the great weakness in the investigation, Ortega can teach professional historians something; indeed a great deal. He can teach us above all the present-day meaning of an eternal problem like that of the death of Rome. He can teach us that a touch of humanism is not out of place in the consideration of this long drawn-out death; the humanism of Ortega, which is completely modern and Spanish and which carries in itself the emotion of the tragedy and the serenity of the narrative. 'I say that the end of a civilization is the scene most imbued with melancholy for men. The possibility that a civilization should die doubles our own mortality.'

The same year in which he had written *La rebelión de las masas* saw the publication of the Italian translation of the work of Guglielmo Ferrero on *La rovina della civiltà antica.* Like Heitland and Ortega, Ferrero attempted an explanation on a politico-constitutional basis; ancient civilization had fallen with the decay of the senatorial assembly which must have ensured legitimacy and in a sense continued the traditions of liberty of the republican epoch. But Ferrero too, like Ortega, was wrong. Recent studies[1] have made clear that the late empire has its own constitutional 'legitimacy'. Again, the estate-owning senators carried enormous weight in the late empire, not only in social life but also in politics. Constantine himself, the founder of the Christian empire, was the emperor who 'restored authority to the senate'. The senate of the late empire presses for laws and approves laws and it often has a part in imperial elections. In the autumn of 397, with a procedure which recalls the republican period, the Roman senate declared Gildo *hostis publicus.* The highest magistrates are always senators, often drawn from ancient senatorial families.[2] At the critical moment of the early fifth century, when Alaric was knocking at the gates of Italy, the wisdom of Stilicho would willingly have appeased him. But it was from the senate that there came the first spark which brought about Stilicho's confusion. A senator cried 'This is not peace but a pact of servitude'. It was a proud protest but made up only of words. He contributed to the overthrow of the Roman leader, but did not succeed in preventing the victory of Alaric.

The problem of liberty is not solely an institutional problem.

[1] Especially Straub, *Vom Herrscherideal in der Spätantike* (1939).

[2] Of course, for magistrates of non-senatorial origin the emperor reserved the traditional right to receive them by means of *adlectio* into the senate (*C. Th.* VI, 4, 10). A characteristic aspect of the increased authority of the senate is the following: under Trajan the substitute consuls 'elected' by the senate were 'made' by the emperor together with the ordinary consuls, before the beginning of their year of office (Pliny, *Pan.*, 61, 5); but in the late empire, since the emperor limited himself to 'accepting' (Symmachus, *ep*, X, 45) the date of the session for the nomination of the *consules suffecti* no longer falls before the beginning of their year of office (it is placed in fact on 9 January, perhaps the date of the contorniate of Thalasius, on which see S. Mazzarino, *Enciclopedia dell'Arte Antica*, II (1959), under *Contorniati*). On the importance of the senate in the late-Roman period see Stroheker, *Der senatorische Adel im spätantiken Gallien* (1948); *Orpheus* (1954), p. 68.

Outside the ancient idea of *libertas*,[1] the Christianity of the persecutions had elaborated a new ideal of liberty. We should not forget that it was a revolution *contra vetustatem*. While in Greek democratic theory the ideal of liberty-democracy had been evolved by contrast with the life of the slave,[2] for the Christian of the age of the persecutions, on the other hand, the new ideal of *libertas* was the common inheritance of both freemen and slaves. In the Passion of Perpetua and Felicitas–one of the most significant documents of Christianity in the age of Septimius Severus–*libertas* is mentioned. But it is not the *libertas* of the ancient Roman republic. It is the common inheritance of slaves and freemen both of whom are present in the group of five martyrs (two slaves and three freemen). The religious ideal of *libertas* could find analogous juridical forms only within narrow limits in the late empire, and these limits mark the most significant aspect of the late-Roman crisis.[3]

[1] Wirszubski, *Libertas* (Italian translation with supplement by Momigliano) (1957).

[2] Aristotle, *Pol.*, VI, 2, 7.

[3] In the same way as Christian *libertas* is distinguished from ancient *libertas*, Christian *dignitas hominis* is distinguished from the ancient idea, e.g., of senatorial *dignitas*; Garin, *La Rinascita* (1938), pp. 102 ff.; Düris, *Reallexikon für Antike und Christentum*, pp. 1024 ff. (1957).

13

Decadence and Continuity

Little by little the twilight of Rome came to appear to many historians between 1920 and 1930 as almost a page of contemporary history. The reference, which was then very frequent, to the events of our own time remains an implication from which it is still difficult today to free ourselves. This is not to be wondered at, for the idea of decadence has always had, more or less, a contemporary reference. When Thucydides in a famous page declared that during the plague 'no one was disposed any longer to devote himself to the ideal (*toi doxanti kaloi*)'[1] he was presenting to us a process of moral disintegration which struck Athens at the heart in a moment of extreme tension. But there he is describing contemporary events and he speaks of a disintegration which was quite limited and circumscribed in time. He does not compare it with other events of a distant age. Plato on the other hand can do this. He makes use of a tradition, which he calls Egyptian,[2] about events nine millennia earlier: the fall of Atlantis. Atlantis had been extended into the sea

[1] Thucydides, II, 53, 3.

[2] Probably they really were. In the Saite period Egyptian culture was penetrated, through the priestly class by Libyan elements and the Libyans could have (even if it seems at first sight strange) preserved an obscure idea of the catastrophe which, as we know today, brought about the end of the Paleolithic age. In this case the Platonic account would reflect traditions connected with the greatest catastrophe of prehistory. For Plato of course the catastrophe of Atlantis was due to the 'decadence' (*exitelos egeneto*) of the divine element among its inhabitants.

and he contrasts this with Athens in very early times, which had lived entirely on the mainland. Thus a leap into mythical prehistory enables him not only to illustrate a cyclical theory but also to give a contemporary significance, in harmony with his conception of the ideal state, to the apocalyptic collapse of a very distant world. What Plato is giving us is a comparison, but one which is only hinted at and hidden, one might say, under the weight of those 9,000 years which stretch into prehistory. After Plato the idea of decadence is given contemporary significance amongst the ancients, in a manner which we might call sociological, in the Aristotelian idea of the corruption which strikes at the ideal forms of the state. We find it applied for instance to the case of Rome in a bitter page of Polybius. And also the idea that states grow old, as a man grows old, always had a contemporary significance.

In the Middle Ages on the other hand the historiographical category of God's judgments gave the element of necessity, continually driven from the past towards the future, to the notion of the end of the empire as the end of the world. The humanists redefined this concept which had been recurrent in ancient history, spoke of the *inclinatio* of the Roman empire and gradually evolved the sixteenth-century idea of *conversiones* which appear in the histories of all states (Bodin) and that of *tempora fatalia* of decadence (Löwenklav). A common concept of the eighteenth century was that of the 'Abnahme' or 'waning' of various political organisms, to be found for instance in the writings of Herder. This is however connected in various ways with the different concept of the tree of life always springing to life again, with many branches, a concept which has a flavour of Dante. Still the idea of 'Abnahme' in Herder was a living idea. It remained a living idea in the nineteenth century with the various theories of phases of culture, the apocalytic forecasts of Lasaulx (inspired by Polybius), and the pessimistic attitude of men like Taine or Seeck or even Wilamowitz. But it was above all in the twentieth century, after the First World War, that the ancient world was transformed into a universe whose death must be regarded as a warning to contemporary society. Wilamowitz had said in 1897: 'Civilization can die, because it has already died once'. In 1926 Rostovtzeff's *History*, which is certainly the masterpiece of recent historiography, went so far, in putting that ancient death of civilization into a contemporary frame of reference, as to make it an archetype for our problems. He ended with the words: 'The evolution of the ancient world has a lesson and a warning for us.' On the other hand forty years ago the Spenglerian conception of historical universes,[1] closed in upon themselves almost like platonic ideas but subject to births and fatal deaths, revealed an almost morbid desire to relive the end of vanished cultures to the last agony.

Would our grandfathers in the nineteenth century[2] have understood this anxiety? They too, as we have just said, felt Herder's old problem of 'Abnahme' and of the various cultures which spring up almost as branches of the ancient tree of human life. They experienced a great revolutionary period, sometimes infected in some of its extreme manifestations by disappointment and sadness. But they never managed to shut up the ancient world in an ideal sarcophagus to contemplate its death with the fear of uncovering there the image of every irreparable disintegration. On the contrary they saw a new life rising from the death of an epoch, in dialectical continuity, as they loved to put it. In Spengler's theory the cycle which closes survives only in forms of pseudomorphosis; that is to say that it vanishes definitively leaving no traces which are not, in the last analysis, illusory or purely exterior. For nineteenth-century men, on the other hand, even for the most pessimistic of them, the life of the spirit continued to stretch forth towards the future. The idea of decadence did not exclude for them the certainty, more than the consolation, of a relative continuity. Amongst the poets of the nineteenth century one especially reached, in his contemplation of historical cycles, the summit of bitterness and even of scepticism; Imre Madách. Nevertheless, in his famous *Az ember tragédiája* ('The Tragedy of Man') published in 1862, the victory of the barbarians over classical civilization is seen in terms of the great Christian imperative, love.[3] He sees new delusions and new errors returning in historical cycles, beginning with the triumph of hate in the new

[1] The 'conflict about Spengler' (Schroeter, *Der Streit um Spengler. Kritik seiner Kritiker* (1922)) is an interesting episode in European culture in the post-war period. Spengler had an enormous influence on both his admirers and his critics, on Eduard Meyer as well as Von Soden.

[2] A characteristic aspect of the nineteenth-century idea of decadence is now illustrated by Pavan, *Rivista Storica Italiana* (1958), pp. 333 ff.

[3] On Madách see especially Vojnovich, *Madách Imre es az Ember Tragédiája* (1914).

Christian society itself. In the end Madách's Adam rejects suicide because life, with its possibility of regeneration, is always stronger than death. The Roman Adam, called Sergiolus in the tragedy, feels like his Eve (Julia), that the imperial age has, through its own refined weariness (what Spengler would call 'civilization'), reached the extreme limit of historical possibility. A new world reveals itself to them when they hear the cry of martyrdom of Christians suffering crucifixion. What Madách wanted to emphasize was the profound contradiction which marks the first three centuries of the empire. The plague also plays a part in his tragedy, and here again he brings out a fact of great historical significance. The plague–which, as we saw, struck terribly at the empire of Marcus Aurelius and Commodus–is itself an agent of renewal. Madách brings the Christian spiritual revolution into the scene in the person of the Apostle Peter. While everyone is fleeing, overcome by terror of the plague, Peter proclaims the message of conversion which will give a new face to ancient civilization and a vision of the barbarian migrations which will trample over the lands of high culture. Nowadays we prefer to express these elements in sociological terms. Toynbee[1] for example would speak of a majority which would no longer allow itself to be led and thus, as an internal proletariat, discovered the higher religion, that is Christianity. Similarly, the barbarians, whom Madách saw trampling down the cultivated fields of classical civilization, would become for Toynbee an uncreative majority, which had however arrived at the stage in which the charm of civilization had come to an end and the 'external proletariat' could give 'victorious responses'. Sociological formulations of this kind seem up-to-date to modern men who accept the theory of cultural cycles subject to an inevitable collapse. They would have been more difficult to conceive in a society like that of the nineteenth century, which had not abandoned the idea of progress even in the midst of the desolation of Adam's many unsuccessful efforts. Still, Toynbee is not Spengler. The fourth decade of this century and after has something which distinguishes it, in spite of the tragedy of the Second World War, from the first post-war period. We cannot, and we never shall again, recover the sense of continuity without reserve; but our faith in

[1] There is a vast literature on Toynbee, as on Spengler. Let it suffice here to recall Vogt, *Saeculum* (1951), pp. 557 ff.

man's creative energy has returned. Today, especially. We tend to oppose to the idea of decadence a new image of what one might call continuity accompanied by a conditional decadence. The condition of it is precisely the new issue, that is the gravity of the encounter with the barbarians who had become soldiers and yet were hated by many members of the Roman ruling class.

When Madách published *The Tragedy of Man* in 1862 the problem of the continuity between the classical world and the Middle Ages was far from new. But, as we have said, it was not a matter of deciding whether there had or had not been a landslide which must have buried the classical world for ever. This would have seemed an extreme statement of the problem to nineteenth-century men. They asked themselves rather whether medieval institutions could be made to go back to the great edifice of classical civilization. Many believed that the barbarians, just because they were barbarians, could not have contributed anything really new. These were questions which sometimes arose from a more or less conscious basis of romantic nationalism, but they were questions which were always of some importance when they were raised by such a man as, for instance, Thierry. Hegel's son devoted his life to them and decided for the originality of medieval institutions. In 1873 Fustel de Coulanges put forward the opposite thesis. He did this at a time which was still coloured for him by the defeat of Sédan. He thought he could demonstrate that the barbarian invasions were of small importance and that Roman continuity was at the source of the institutions of France. According to him, it was not the decadence and weakness of the empire which had brought about the catastrophe but, on the contrary, the weakness of the Germans. Roman life, in compensation, continued. Something of the same sort was then maintained, as far as continuity was concerned, by L. M. Hartmann. In our century the study of this problem reached a climax between the First and Second World Wars. Two outstanding scholars, and their schools, maintained that the barbarian migrations did not offer any solution to the problem of continuity. These were the Austrian Dopsch and the Belgian Pirenne.[1] It is an

[1] Dopsch, *The Economic and Social Foundations of European Civilisation* (1937); Pirenne, *Mohammed and Charlemagne* (1939).

interesting, and, at first sight, also strange phenomenon that the first post-war period expressed in these two medievalists the tendency to postpone the end of the ancient world until the age of Charlemagne or at least until the Arab invasion, while at the same time emphasizing, in the work of ancient historians like Rostovtzeff or philosophers of history like Spengler, the existence of a crisis of the ancient world as early as the Roman imperial epoch.[1]

How do we see this problem of continuity today?

The first thing to be said in reply is that we have to make a distinction, indeed many distinctions. If one speaks of continuity as such, in a general way, one cannot follow the changing complexity of the phenomena which presents themselves to the eye of the historian. In a general sense the great estate and the 'vassalage' of the late empire (the *vassi* are the Gallic peasants who take refuge in the patronage of lords) continue, of course, with new Germanic structures, in the feudal society of the West. But, in terms of concrete examples, where the Germanic settlement was comparatively heavy, it was just the villas that were abandoned, while cities and fortified settlements continued to drag out their life. One finds that such cities as Colonia, Vangiones, Nemetes and Argentoratum continue to lead an active life, in a space which has now been narrowed down, though it had already become narrow after the third century invasions. One calls Nemetes by the name Speyer and one prefers Strasburg to Argentoratum, but they are still the same old cities. The old lords however have abandoned their villas in these regions of the old Roman province of Germania. In southern Gaul, on the other hand, life continued without any real break of continuity. This continuity was already emphasized by the Byzantine historian Agathias in the age of Justinian; and the same was true of course of Italy also. In the Danube provinces however continuity was broken several times. Life sometimes withdrew from the city, where this survived, into the suburbs, a phenomenon which occurs also in the cities of the old Roman Germania.[2] Pannonia was now stripped of its peasants who,

[1] An analogous observation, with a penetrating explanation of this historiographical confusion, is made by Straub, *Historia* (1950), p. 53.

[2] Ewig, *Congresso Internazionale delle Scienze Storiche, Relazioni*, VI (1955), pp. 561 ff. (especially, pp. 588 ff.); Székely, *Tanulmányok Budapest Múltyából* (1957), p. 7.

as rebels, had united themselves with the barbarians to move against Gaul in 406. To a great extent it had to construct its life anew, with different blood in the old veins, to use the words of Madách.

14

Criticism of the Idea of Decadence

From the end of the nineteenth century onwards the idea of decadence became, so to speak, bivalent. On the one side it bore with it a desolate picture of decline, following the long tradition which runs from the humanists to the romantics. Today, however, the idea of decadence also contains a suggestion of sympathy for all the refined and complex things which the great civilizations can produce in their late epochs. This second aspect of the old idea is in a sense a revelation made by modern poetry. It asserts itself especially in the last decades of the nineteenth century. At that time, while historians like Taine and Seeck were excited by the great tragedies of humanity and Seeck was speaking of the 'elimination of the best', poets, without being aware of it themselves, were pointing out a new way. Ten years before Seeck published his *History*, the end of the Roman Empire inspired in Verlaine his famous manifesto for a new literary movement, the sonnet entitled *Langueur* which begins with the line *Je suis l'Empire à la fin de la décadence*. Verlaine saw the 'white barbarians' overturn the Roman empire by their bloody acts of war, and art at the same time withdrawing into its solitude–the almost abstract, as it were, form of a luminous civilization.

Je suis l'Empire à la fin de la décadence,
Qui regarde passer les grands Barbares blancs
En composant des acrostiches indolents
D'un style d'or où la langueur du soleil danse.

L'âme seulette a mal au coeur d'un ennui dense.
Là-bas on dit qu'il est de longs combats sanglants.
O n'y pouvoir, étant si faible aux voeux si lents,
O n'y vouloir fleurir un peu cette existence!

O n'y vouloir, ô n'y pouvoir mourir un peu!
Ah! tout est bu! Bathylle, as-tu fini de rire?
Ah! tout est bu, tout est mangé! Plus rien à dire!

Seul, un poème un peu niais qu'on jette au feu,
Seul, un esclave un peu coureur qui vous néglige,
Seul, un ennui d'on ne sait quoi qui vous afflige!

This supreme utterance of 'décadentisme' came from 1883. The word 'décadentisme' did not greatly please Verlaine and his friends –as is well known it was abbreviated to 'décadisme'. It encouraged in fact the idea of a decadence full of contradictions and melancholy but almost proud of itself. These were the perplexities of an old conception introduced into a world which was looking for a new experience. The centuries-old pessimistic idea of decline had seemed to be an unalterable inheritance; but Verlaine, who had written amongst other things about the martyrdom of the Christians struggling against the old paganism ('the red ecstasy of the first Christian under the ravening teeth'), could not accept, without more or less unconscious limitations, the idea that the Christian empire had been an age of decline. Not only his Catholicism but also his poetic intuition rebelled against this idea. The 'white barbarians', towards whom Verlaine saw the dying empire turning its eyes, were the same as the *barbares blancs aux yeux bleus*, whom he had also in another composition contrasted with the 'tender' Ovid, an illustrious exile in the midst of barbarians who drive fabulous herds.

The decadence of the Roman empire, as Verlaine saw it in 1883, was made up then not only of weariness but also of the superior consciousness of a civilization which is not unworthy of itself. Verlaine was looking, as he said in the celebrated letter to Anatole Baju, for something which would set aside the *idée abaissante de décadence*. Nevertheless, in spite of these convictions, his poetic theory led, in the developments which he would often have condemned, to symbolism and to disharmony made into music. The appeal to the end of the Roman empire is interesting just for this: that the idea of decadence vanished before the approval with which the poet exalted the superiority of ancient culture in its last golden style. 'Everything has been drunk' and there is nothing more to say, but that late-Roman languor is the languor of the sun and it takes its place aristocratically among the acrostics from the golden style. (As early as 562, indeed, the Byzantine poet Paulus Silentiarius had said that 'the golden mosaic of St. Sophia shines so brightly as almost to make us see the midday sun in spring when it gilds every mountain peak.')

Nowadays we understand well enough this exaltation of the late-Roman light in works of representational art and, as Verlaine wanted to emphasize, of poetic creation in general. From humanistic times onwards, up to the time in which Verlaine was writing, the culture of the late empire had appeared to be *qualitatively* inferior to that of the preceding ages of high Roman culture. For Lorenzo Valla the decline of the empire was already synonymous with the decline of the arts. In 1787 Friedrich August Wolf thought to find in the progressive loss of poetic 'simplicity' the cause of the Roman literary crisis after Hadrian. Bernhardy said something similar again in 1830, with the important correction that the crisis began in the age of Commodus (180–92) about half a century after Hadrian. Even the great Burckhardt did not appreciate the literature of the late empire.

As everyone knows, the tendency to underestimation has survived even to the present day through the influence of textbooks or through conventional prejudices. The 'decadentist' literary movement, which exalted the golden style in which the languor of the sun dances, therefore brought about a radical change of attitude. A new era in the interpretation of late-Roman poetry began. Des Esseintes, Huysman's hero, loves the powerful primitiveness of the greatest Christian poet of the third century, Commodian. The art of the decadents itself has some similarity with the requirements of the late empire, striving for liberation from the quantitative schemes which savour of the logos. Even if it does not strike us so, the revision of the traditional schemes in late-Roman literature was therefore analogous to the new poetic art of decadentism. It is now a scholarly revision, which is officially accepted and has penetrated into the university lecture-rooms. Who could remain unmoved today before a page of Commodian or Ammianus or St. Augustine? All the voices of the 'decadent' Roman world, pagan or Christian, from the third to the fifth centuries, have been made accessible to us. The cultivated Des Esseintes, in 1883, was a pioneer of the evaluation which today seems obvious.

The same may be said (in this case we are revealing nothing unexpected since the comparison was made long ago) of the relation between contemporary representational arts and the modern evaluation of late-Roman painting, sculpture and architecture. At any rate no one could dissociate the rebellious climate of modern expressionism from the mastering of late-Roman aesthetic values in the work of Alois Riegl and in that of Franz Wickhoff. After the writings of these two Austrian masters and the more recent elaborations of their theories, we now recognize a stylistic sensibility in late-Roman art as lively as any other and also quite new and revealing: 'the representation' said Riegl, 'of the individual form in infinite space'. We may conclude that decadentism and expressionism and other categories of modern literary and art criticism are paths of understanding which lead to the late-Roman world. 'Decadence', said Riegl, 'does not exist.'

Lovers of pure form and of rational perspective will of course continue to prefer classical to late-Roman art. Ludwig Curtius may be taken as a representative of them. But it may also be added that the conflict between the classicists like Curtius and the followers of Riegl is not irreconcilable. On the contrary, the drawing together of ourselves and the late-Roman world, in so far as both epochs express disturbance and irreparable uncertainty, is a point on which all can agree. Let us imagine a conversation with an unyielding classicist. He will point out, for instance, that the walls of besieged cities do not fall to the ground at the push of a soldier, as seems to happen in a scene on the arch of Constantine. Criticisms of this kind do not seem new because we hear similar ones every day in relation to some painting or other by Chagall or Picasso. At bottom we all know that the traditionalists have a reason for their enjoyment of the old proportions. And in the same way the artists on the other hand have to give expression to their own time even to the extent of discovering an apparently absurd perspective. In the age which saw the decline of ancient culture there were also, in poetry and in the figural arts, classicizing 'shapers', like the poet Claudian[1] in some of his compositions or certain masters of jewellery, who could produce creations which still stir our admiration. But the new age expressed itself in a sort of structural abstractionism which resulted, of course, from the abolition of the classical.[2] We have no right to impose on an age the representational standards which were proper to another.

How far can the revaluation of late-Roman poetry and art be extended to the social and political manifestations of the late empire? Our own age has undoubtedly acquired an aesthetic sensibility which is receptive to the new creative forms expressed in the mosaics of the Piazza Armerina or in the colossal head of Constantine in the Museo dei Conservatori. Still we must not forget that if we extend these presuppositions to the expressions of the whole of late-Roman life we run the risk of missing the central point of one of our problems: the barbarization of the western part of Roman empire about the sixth century and the loss of Syria and Egypt in the seventh century. We may, and perhaps we ought to, reject the word 'decadence', as far as the literature and art of the late empire are concerned, and we may be persuaded by a certain *pruderie* to avoid using that terminology for the other phenomena of late-Roman life. But we have no right to condemn without a hearing those historians who insist on the crisis of the empire in the political and social field.

The fall of the empire in the west is always there to remind us that late-Roman Spain, Gaul and Italy were succeeded by a world of Goths, Merovingians and Lombards. Undoubtedly there was a discontinuity as violent as a clash of continents. If one places an extreme emphasis upon the gravity of this clash, one may go on to the conclusion that it was only barbarian violence, rather than any internal crisis, which could destroy the solid structure of ancient civilization. This extreme solution of the problem, a solution which however can illuminate only one aspect of it, has been put forward in a book by André Piganiol which has now become a classic.

[1] Klingner, *Römische Geisteswelt* (1943), pp. 359 ff.; Schmid, *Reallexikon für Antike und Christentum*, III (1955), pp. 155 ff. Cf. further the judgment of Huysmans, *A Rebours*, pp. 46–7.

[2] The interest of late-Roman people in the novel has been compared with the modern interest by Altheim, *Roman und Dekadenz* (1951) (cf. Brelich, *Gnomon* (1952), p. 163). Some sentiments of late-Roman Christian poetry are compared with our existentialism by E. Rapisarda, *Misc. Studi Lett. Crist. ant.*, III (1951), pp. 136 ff.

'It is a mistake to say that Rome was decadent. Plundered and disfigured by the barbarian invaders of the third century it rose again from its ruins. At the same time and at the cost of a great crisis it carried through a labour of internal transformation. A new conception of imperial power was formed, the Byzantine; a new conception of truth and beauty, the medieval; a new conception of collective and joint work in the service of society. None of the ills from which the empire suffered, the fiscal exactions, the subversion of the fortunes of the social classes, originated in this fruitful travail of change. They all derived from the continual war carried on by disorganized bands of Germans who had managed to live for centuries and centuries on the frontiers of the empire still without becoming civilized. It is too easy to suppose that when the barbarians got into the empire everything was dead and that is was a powerless body, a corpse soaked in blood, [these are Herder's famous words] or indeed that the Roman empire of the West was not destroyed by a brutal attack and simply dozed off. Roman civilization did not die a natural death. It was murdered. *La civilisation romaine n'est pas morte de sa belle mort. Elle a été assassinée.*'[1]

These words of Piganiol take us back to the beginning of every inquiry into Roman decadence and indeed every inquiry into decadence in general. Polybius said that two causes of death struck at states, the interior cause and the exterior cause. He had also foreseen both these causes operating for Rome; the first, he thought, already definable, the second indefinable. We are used to describing as decadence what Polybius called the internal cause. While the first post-war period predominantly laid stress on the internal decadence (for example in the philosopher Spengler and the historian Rostovtzeff) and was only occasionally inclined to dwell on the barbarian *mainmise*, the second post-war period in contrast has issued through Piganiol a general denial of the idea of decadence similar to that which had been supported for the aesthetic aspects by Riegl. According to this conception the barbarians tore to pieces an empire which was still full of life. The idea of a fatal outcome following barbarian violence is substituted for the idea of a crisis.

We have already said that Piganiol's formula in certain respects

[1] Piganiol, *L'Empire Chrétien* (1947), pp. 421–2, in conflict with Sundwall, *Weströmische Studien* (1915), p. 19. Cf. Ensslin, *Gnomon* (1949), p. 253.

hits the truth. We may repeat that the age of the death of Rome threw up individuals of great stature, sometimes giants: Constantine, Julian the Apostate, Stilicho. Technical innovations and the application of centuries-old discoveries, which had been neglected up to that time, make it clear that we are not dealing with a world that has fallen asleep. But this is not enough to disperse the shadows which lie over the social structure of the empire in that late epoch. Men felt themselves oppressed by the bureaucracy. The peasants did not love the state to which they belonged. They took refuge in the patronage of powerful men to escape from the tributes. The invasion of the barbarians is thus inseparable from the internal difficulties. They are a single phenomenon with two faces. The criticism of the idea of decadence may then be incorporated into our theory by making a distinction. We can say that there is no decadence where the spirit of late-Roman man moves more freely, in the fields of poetry or art or religious life, and also perhaps in the intimate recesses of his home life and its effects. There is however a crisis in those things which concern the state, the *res publica exinanita* as the men of Julian's circle called it. The literature and art of the late empire are, as we have seen, expressions of an intuitive sensibility of a high order which can still move or exalt us. But there was a political and social crisis even if there was not a general decadence. The great creators lived in the midst of a civilization which left them solitary or which felt weary, although it displays to us infinite spiritual resources. The Roman empire was struck dead by the barbarians. But only structures which are already cracking give up wearily under a blow struck violently from without.

Polybius was substantially right when he proposed two causes for the fall of the Roman state and for the fall of states in general. We may replace 'causes' by 'aspects', or some similar word which is more acceptable to modern ways of thought, but in any case the ruin of the Roman empire appears to us in this double sense. From Flavio Biondo onwards for five centuries there were frequent attempts to give prominence to the 'internal cause' which almost forgot that the barbarians too did play a part in the collapse and in the transformation of the empire. Now that the myth of late-Roman artistic decadence may be regarded as exploded, our insight is fuller. The ruin of the ancient world is a tragedy with many voices. We are watching the failure of balance between the requirements of supranational centralization and productive inadequacy, the separation of certain 'nations', and the related victory of barbarians of many races in regions which classical civilization had attached to the Greco-Roman heart of the empire. Only if we hold *all* these phenomena in our minds can we grasp the theme which gives the drama its unity.

On both the chronological and the cultural planes the final collapse of the Roman empire in the west was preceded by the formation and collapse of another empire which may also be called supranational, Attila's empire of the Huns. This however was a supranational empire of nomads, in contrast to the great sedentary civilization of the classical peoples. The Hun empire occupied Pannonia, a great area which had formerly been Roman, and outside the old Roman empire its dominion stretched in astonishing vastness from the Volga to the Rhine. The Romans were greatly impressed by its supranational character. In 451 the great federation of tribes ruled by the Huns moved like an unexpected tornado towards Gaul. A Roman poet described it in this way:

'The whole barbarian world is coming together from the North, the aggressive Rugii together with the Geloni and followed by the truculent Gepidi, the Scythians, Burgundians, Huns, the Bellonoti, the Neuri, the Bastarnae, the Thuringians, the Bructeri, the Franks who are washed by the waves of the Neckar in which seaweed grows. The wild Hercynian Forest, torn by the battle-axe, has been transformed into rafts and has filled the Rhine with planks.'

Attila himself, the leader of this horde, understood the historical significance of his attempt at a supranational creation, but he was too bound to the nomadic premises of its creation. The genius of this terrible and yet human man was equal to the boldest encounters. In 451, he withdrew from the Gallic campaign after the battle of the Catalaunian Plains but in 452 he fell upon Italy and cruelly plundered Aquileia. He reached Milan. In that city he saw a painting which represented the two Roman emperors, Valentinian III and Marcian, on thrones of gold with the Huns defeated and lying at their feet. Milan was the symbol of that vitality which makes us doubtful about 'decadence' and, in spite of the Hun menace, there were still painters in that industrious city. Impressed by the sight of this representation, which seemed to him like an insult, Attila had another picture painted in which he was enthroned and the Roman emperors were bringing gold to his feet. This whimsical pride, however, did not even then suggest to him a political plan of broad historical significance. He never imagined the possibility of replacing the empire of the Romans with the empire of the Huns.

His imagination was dominated by gold but could not advance beyond this. It did not occur to him that he could use his gold to construct the economy of his state on a civic basis. He remained to the end the man who had dreamt of conquering the gold of the Rhine and who had ordered the Milanese painters to represent the Roman emperors bearing gold to the lord of the Huns. After his death, which occurred in 453, some of the subject peoples rebelled and with the battle of the Nedâo (a river in Pannonia) the nomad empire of the Huns disappeared.

Some very recent studies[1] have attempted to investigate more deeply the phenomenon of this meteoric Hun empire which vanished with its extraordinary leader. One striking aspect of the Hun crisis is the difficulty of founding a nomad supranational state in competition, so to speak, with the Roman state, at a time when the latter (based on an age-old bureaucratic centralization) was giving way in the west to centrifugal forces of demonic intensity.

Forty years earlier the Visigoth Ataulf had renounced the formation of a *Gothia* in place of Romania and had established, though he was the successor of Alaric and the husband of Galla Placidia, a sort of national Gothic state. Now in 453, the death of Attila, who had also not thought of replacing the old Romania with a new Hunnia, revealed to his successors the contradictions in a very obscure situation. It was possible to strike at the Roman supranational state at vital points but it was preposterous to found a barbarian supranational state on a permanent basis. On the other hand the Huns had the additional difficulty of creating a Hun national state, a difficulty which the Goths did not have to face. A federation of tribes could

[1] Thompson, *A History of Attila and the Huns* (1948); Altheim, *Attila und die Hunnen* (1951); Harmatta, *Recherches Internationales à la lumière du Marxisme* (Mai-Juin 1957), pp. 179 ff.

dissolve but a compact national unity could provide, as it did in the case of the Goths, the nucleus for the construction of a solid and permanent state.

The political dissolution of the Roman empire, which began at the end of the fourth century and was already plain in the fifth, the century of Ataulf, Genseric, Attila, Odoacer and Theodoric, was completed in the seventh century by the Arabs. In the course of this long series of events, stretching over more than 200 years, the empire was dispossessed of Pannonia, Gaul, Spain, the Lombard regions in Italy, Syria, Egypt and Africa. Nothing stirs the imagination of the historian so much as the reduction of a vast political unit to manageable proportions. The Roman empire, in its immense extent from the Euphrates to the Atlantic and from the Danube to the Sahara, had accustomed men for centuries to a reality in which the division between the possible and the impossible was not recognized.

Essential Bibliography

The following list contains, in chronological order (of the dates of first publication, not of the editions cited here), comprehensive works relating to the late empire or to the idea of decadence. References to works dealing with particular problems are given in the footnotes to the body of the book.

GODEFROY (GOTHOFREDUS), *Codex Theodosianus cum perpetuis commentariis Johannis Gothofredi*, ed. Ritter (1736 ff.).

TILLEMONT, *Histoire des Emperors et des Autres Princes*, I–VI (on the late Empire in the strict sense, IV–VI) (1690 ff.).

LEBEAU, *Histoire du Bas-Empire*, I–XXVIII (1752 ff.).

GIBBON, *The History of the Decline and Fall of the Roman Empire*, ed. Bury (1909–14).

SEECK, *Geschichte des Untergangs der antiken Welt*, I–VI (1921).

VASILIEV, *History of the Byzantine Empire, 324–1453*, English trans., second edition (1952).

SPENGLER, *The Decline of the West*, trans. C. F. Atkinson (1926).

ROSTOVTZEFF, *Social and Economic History of the Roman Empire*, second edition, revised by P. M. Fraser (1957).

LOT, *The End of the Ancient World and the Beginnings of the Middle Ages*, English trans. (1931); *Les Invasions Germaniques* (1935).

STEIN, *Geschichte des spätrömischen Reiches* (1928); French trans. as *Histoire du Bas Empire* by J.-R. Palanque (1949–59).

REHM, *Der Untergang Roms in abendländischen Denken* (1930).

SOLARI, *Il Rinnovamento dell'Impero Romano*, I–II (1938).

WERNER, *Der Untergang Roms, Studien zum Dekadenzproblem in der Antiken Geistesgeschichte* (1939).

OSTROGORSKY, *History of the Byzantine State*, trans. J. M. Hussey (1956).

PARIBENI, *Da Diocleziano alla Caduta dell'Impero d'Occidente* (1941).
TOYNBEE, *A Study of History* (1934–54).
PIGANIOL, *L'Empire Chrétien* (1947).

The most recent survey of problems of the late Empire has been provided by Vogt, *Speculum* (1958) and the most recent studies of the idea of decadence by Pavan, *Rivista Storica Italiana* (1958) and Sasso, *Ibid.* (pp. 333 ff.). The most recent work on the history of the concept of the barbarian migrations and on the migrations themselves is Helbling, *Goten und Wandalen* (1957). The reader should of course consult the big general works such as *The Cambridge Ancient History*, XII, and *The Cambridge Medieval History*, I; the *Reallexikon für Antike und Christentum* (1941 ff.); general histories of Rome which include the late empire, e.g., Piganiol, *Histoire de Rome*, Mashkin (now available in German translation), Kovaliov (now in Italian translation), Giannelli-Mazzarino, Aymard, etc. A deeper study of the third century is essential because this period, or rather the period from Commodus onwards, may be regarded on the cultural plane as late empire. See the general works of Besnier and Calderini and Altheim's, *Niedergang*, I–II. Also histories of Rome which do not include the late empire are useful for the problem of the crisis of the ancient world. I should like to close this book, indeed, with a passage taken from the epilogue to Ferrabino's *Nuova Storia di Roma* (I–III, 1942–7, up to Trajan) which expresses clearly the modern sensitivity to the theme of Roman decadence.

'At that time [A.D. 100] there was a dual feeling of a perfection which had been achieved and of an inevitable decadence. . . . The Patricians were blamed for an excess of wars and the excess of riches: the middle class for an excess of peace which had become a fault and an evil. Who pronounced these judgments? Classical culture in the name of the conscience of humanity–not so that condemnation should follow the judgment but so that its own capacity for perpetuation and redemption should outweigh the guilt' (Ferrabino, op. cit., III, 666 ff.).

Index

A Note about the Author

SANTO MAZZARINO, the distinguished Professor of Ancient History at the University of Catania and holder of many other positions of importance in the academic and intellectual world, is the author of six major historical works on Greek, Roman, and Mediterranean history besides *The End of the Ancient World*, editor of two learned journals, and a leading member of many learned societies. He was born in Catania, Italy, in 1916, and educated there at the Classical School and the University, from which he received his degree of "Laureate in Letters and Philosophy" in 1936. Professor Mazzarino lives in Rome and Catania with his wife, the former Lady Vera Stalteri, and two children.

April 1966

The text of this book is set in Monotype Ehrhardt No. 453
Printed in offset by Halliday Lithograph Corp., West Hanover, Mass.
Bound by The Book Press, Brattleboro, Vt.